JOHN

FACE-TO-FACE WITH JESUS

WOODROW KROLL

CROSSWAY BOOKS

A PUBLISHING MINISTRY OF
GOOD NEWS PUBLISHERS
WHEATON, ILLINOIS

CH		17	16	15	14	13	12	11	10	09	08	07
15	14	13	12	11	10	9	8	7	6	5	4	3	2	1

Table of Contents

How to Use This Study

Your study of John will have maximum impact if you prayerfully read each day's Scripture passage. The entire text of John from the English Standard Version is printed before each lesson's reading, so that everything you need is in one place. While we recommend reading the Scripture passage before you read the devotional, some have found it helpful to use the devotional as preparation for reading the Scripture. If you are unfamiliar with the English Standard Version (on which this series of studies is based), you might consider reading the devotional, followed by reading the passage again from a different Bible text. This will give you an excellent basis for considering the rest of the lesson.

After each devotional there are three sections designed to help you better understand and apply the lesson's Scripture passage.

Consider It—Several questions will help you unpack and reflect on the Scripture passage of the day. These could be used for a small group discussion.

Express It—Suggestions for turning the insights from the lesson into prayer.

Go Deeper—The nature of this study makes it important to see the Book of John in the context of other passages and insights from Scripture. This brief section will allow you to consider some of the implications of the day's passage for the central theme of the study (Face-to-Face with Jesus) as well as the way it fits with the rest of Scripture.

Meet the Word

Those who read the Gospels in order can't miss the distinct change in style within the first few verses of John's Gospel. Matthew, Mark and Luke prepare us for John. As we begin this study, get ready for an up close and personal experience with Jesus Christ.

John 1:1–51

The Word Became Flesh

1 In the beginning was the Word, and the Word was with God, and the Word was God. [2]He was in the beginning with God. [3]All things were made through him, and without him was not any thing made that was made. [4]In him was life, and the life was the light of men. [5]The light shines in the darkness, and the darkness has not overcome it.

[6]There was a man sent from God, whose name was John. [7]He came as a witness, to bear witness about the light, that all might believe through him. [8]He was not the light, but came to bear witness about the light.

Key Verse

But to all who did receive him, who believed in his name, he gave the right to become children of God (John 1:12).

[9]The true light, which enlightens everyone, was coming into the world. [10]He was in the world, and the world was made through him, yet the world did not know him. [11]He came to his own, and his own people did not receive him. [12]But to all who did receive him, who believed in his name, he gave the right to become children of God, [13]who were born, not of blood nor of the will of the flesh nor of the will of man, but of God.

[14]And the Word became flesh and dwelt among us, and we have seen his glory, glory as of the only Son from the Father, full of grace and truth. [15](John bore witness about him, and cried out, "This was he of whom I said, 'He who comes after me ranks before me, because he was before me.'") [16]And from his fullness we have all received, grace upon grace. [17]For the law was given through Moses; grace and truth came through Jesus Christ. [18]No one has ever seen God; the only God, who is at the Father's side, he has made him known.

The Testimony of John the Baptist

[19]And this is the testimony of John, when the Jews sent priests and Levites from Jerusalem to ask him, "Who are you?" [20]He confessed, and did not deny, but confessed, "I am not the Christ." [21]And they asked him, "What then? Are you Elijah?" He said, "I am not." "Are you the Prophet?" And he answered, "No." [22]So they said to him, "Who are you? We need to give an answer to those who sent us. What do you say about yourself?" [23]He said, "I am the voice of one crying out in the wilderness, 'Make straight the way of the Lord,' as the prophet Isaiah said."

[24](Now they had been sent from the Pharisees.) [25]They asked him, "Then why are you baptizing, if you are neither the Christ, nor Elijah, nor the Prophet?" [26]John answered them, "I baptize with water, but among you stands one you do not know, [27]even he who comes after me, the strap of whose sandal I am not worthy to untie." [28]These things took place in Bethany across the Jordan, where John was baptizing.

Behold, the Lamb of God

[29]The next day he saw Jesus coming toward him, and said, "Behold, the Lamb of God, who takes away the sin of the world!

30This is he of whom I said, 'After me comes a man who ranks before me, because he was before me.' 31I myself did not know him, but for this purpose I came baptizing with water, that he might be revealed to Israel." 32And John bore witness: "I saw the Spirit descend from heaven like a dove, and it remained on him. 33I myself did not know him, but he who sent me to baptize with water said to me, 'He on whom you see the Spirit descend and remain, this is he who baptizes with the Holy Spirit.' 34And I have seen and have borne witness that this is the Son of God."

Jesus Calls the First Disciples

35The next day again John was standing with two of his disciples, 36and he looked at Jesus as he walked by and said, "Behold, the Lamb of God!" 37The two disciples heard him say this, and they followed Jesus. 38Jesus turned and saw them following and said to them, "What are you seeking?" And they said to him, "Rabbi" (which means Teacher), "where are you staying?" 39He said to them, "Come and you will see." So they came and saw where he was staying, and they stayed with him that day, for it was about the tenth hour. 40One of the two who heard John speak and followed Jesus was Andrew, Simon Peter's brother. 41He first found his own brother Simon and said to him, "We have found

the Messiah" (which means Christ). 42He brought him to Jesus. Jesus looked at him and said, "So you are Simon the son of John? You shall be called Cephas" (which means Peter).

Jesus Calls Philip and Nathanael

43The next day Jesus decided to go to Galilee. He found Philip and said to him, "Follow me." 44Now Philip was from Bethsaida, the city of Andrew and Peter. 45Philip found Nathanael and said to him, "We have found him of whom Moses in the Law and also the prophets wrote, Jesus of Nazareth, the son of Joseph." 46Nathanael said to him, "Can anything good come out of Nazareth?" Philip said to him, "Come and see." 47Jesus saw Nathanael coming toward him and said of him, "Behold, an Israelite indeed, in whom there is no deceit!" 48Nathanael said to him, "How do you know me?" Jesus answered him, "Before Philip called you, when you were under the fig tree, I saw you." 49Nathanael answered him, "Rabbi, you are the Son of God! You are the King of Israel!" 50Jesus answered him, "Because I said to you, 'I saw you under the fig tree,' do you believe? You will see greater things than these." 51And he said to him, "Truly, truly, I say to you, you will see heaven opened, and the angels of God ascending and descending on the Son of Man."

Go Deeper

This lesson's key verse introduces two words that will appear repeatedly in the Gospel of John: *receive* (see John 1:11–12; 3:11, 27; 5:34, 41, 43–44; 7:39; 12:48; 14:17; 20:22) and *believe* (see John 1:7, 12, 50; 3:12, 18; 4:21, 42, 48; 5:38, 44, 46–47; 6:29–30, 36, 64; 8:24, 30, 45–46; 9:35–36, 38; 10:25–26, 37–38; 11:15, 26, 40, 42, 48; 12:36, 39, 44; 13:19; 14:1, 10–11, 29; 16:9, 30–31; 17:20–21; 19:35; 20:25, 31).

(continued)

Go Deeper Continued ...

John uses one term to explain the other. To *receive* Jesus means to "*believe* in his name." *Receive* means more than opening a package or mail. It can also mean to acknowledge, welcome or honor. In formal settings, when one person accepts a visit from someone, we say they "received" their guest.

Believe means more than mental agreement; it means active trust. From the beginning of this Gospel we are being asked not simply to admit Jesus is God, but to treat Him as God by the way we act, trust and live. This day-by-day decision will become clearer as we make our way through the Gospel of John.

The Gospel of John ranks high in the list of favorite Bible books. Many followers of Jesus cite passages in this book as the key words of truth that awakened them spiritually. Others value the life-changing encounters John recorded between Jesus and people like Nicodemus, the woman at the well, the woman caught in adultery and the man born blind. They see themselves in these conversations and find in them a Savior worth knowing.

And practically every believer in Jesus knows John 3:16. The frequent appearance of that reference at football games probably doesn't do much to tell people about Jesus, but it does provoke a smile of recognition in believers. And occasionally someone may innocently ask, "What's that JOHN 3:16 all about? I see it everywhere." Now, that's an opportunity to share your faith.

Your study of the Gospel of John will probably take you through familiar territory. But if this is the first time you have studied one of Jesus' biographies on your own, be ready for some surprises. The Jesus you have heard about will meet you in these pages. And whatever you've heard, He will be greater, better and more challenging than you expect.

In this lesson's passage, the apostle gives a resounding "Yes!" answer to a question that was as prevalent in the first century as it is today: Is Jesus really God? This is also John's answer to the question Jesus asked in Matthew 16:15, "But who do you say that I am?" On that occasion, Peter answered for all the disciples. Years later, John gave the short answer to the same question in John 1:1: "In the beginning was the Word, and the Word was with God, and the Word was God." He offered us the long version of the answer to the question with his entire Gospel.

In a way, John's approach is similar to the beginning of the Bible in Genesis 1. There, Moses did not start with a need to prove God's existence; he began by declaring that the existence of everything else simply makes God a necessary belief. Likewise, John doesn't set out to prove Jesus is God; he declares Jesus is God and then proceeds to demonstrate his point. Both Genesis and John remind us that "in the beginning" Someone already was. Someone orchestrated the beginning. God, the Word who has no beginning, started everything else.

People who deny God's existence reveal one or more insights about themselves. When they use the term "God," they are already admitting they have an idea about God, but they are choosing to reject it. The real problem isn't with God but with their distorted view of God. When someone mentions doubts or denial of God's existence, ask them to describe the God they don't believe in. Tell them that in all likelihood you don't believe in that god either. But be ready with an answer if they ask you the same question: "Well, tell me about the God you believe in." Be ready to talk about Jesus.

People who deny that Jesus is God usually try to mix a little respect with their rejection. They offer compliments with a "but" attached: "Jesus was a great teacher *but* not God," or "Jesus was one of God's spokesmen *but* not God." As has been pointed out in many ways, we can't avoid Jesus by being nice to Him. He won't settle for partial commitments.

Jesus was a great teacher, but He said too many things that a great teacher *wouldn't* say unless He was also God. Jesus spoke, not as God's spokesman, but as God. He did not expect compliments from men and women; He expected to be received as Lord and as God. This lesson's key verse makes the choice clear: reject or receive. Those who don't receive have rejected, even if

> **❝** *Jesus spoke, not as God's spokesman, but as God. He did not expect compliments from men and women; He expected to be received as Lord and as God.* **❞**

they have done so nicely. "But to all who did receive him, who believed in his name, he gave the right to become children of God" (John 1:12).

During this study of the Gospel of John, you will have the opportunity to make this choice about Jesus or confirm the choice you made previously in life. We trust that as you come face-to-face with Jesus, you will understand in a new and deep way what it means to receive Him and believe in His name.

Express It

The phrase "In Jesus' name" that believers often use to end their prayers comes from the Gospel of John (16:24). When we use this expression in prayer, we are stating that we have Christ's permission to ask. Our thoughts and requests come "under His signature." We don't talk to God based on our worthiness but upon Christ's. As you pray today, think about the high honor of having permission to address your Creator.

Consider It
As you read John 1:1–51, consider these questions:

1) In what ways is it clear that "Word" refers to Jesus in this chapter?

_____

_____

_____

_____

2) Matthew and Luke have lengthy descriptions of Jesus' birth. How does John 1:14 describe Jesus' arrival?

_____

_____

_____

_____

3) How many names or qualities of Jesus can you find in this chapter?

_____

_____

_____

_____

4) In what ways other than already mentioned does John 1 parallel Genesis 1?

_____

_____

_____

_____

5) How important do you think it is to answer the question, "Is Jesus God"?

_____

_____

_____

_____

6) What is your answer, and what difference has that answer made in your life?

_____

_____

_____

_____

The Life of the Party

Jesus knew when to be restrained and when to be radical. He transformed a wedding party and demolished a shopping mall. In this lesson, we'll see the extremes of the "Jesus effect." His visits always made a difference—one way or another.

John 2:1–25

The Wedding at Cana

2 On the third day there was a wedding at Cana in Galilee, and the mother of Jesus was there. [2]Jesus also was invited to the wedding with his disciples. [3]When the wine ran out, the mother of Jesus said to him, "They have no wine." [4]And Jesus said to her, "Woman, what does this have to do with me? My hour has not yet come." [5]His mother said to the servants, "Do whatever he tells you."

[6]Now there were six stone water jars there for the Jewish rites of purification, each holding twenty or thirty gallons. [7]Jesus said to the servants, "Fill the jars with water." And they filled them up to the brim. [8]And he said to them, "Now draw some out and take it to the master of the feast." So they took it. [9]When the master of the feast tasted the water now become wine, and did not know where it came from (though the servants who had drawn the water knew), the master of the feast called the bridegroom [10]and said to him, "Everyone serves the good wine first, and when people have drunk freely, then the poor wine. But you have kept the good wine until now." [11]This, the first of his signs, Jesus did at Cana in Galilee, and manifested his glory. And his disciples believed in him.

[12]After this he went down to Capernaum, with his mother and his brothers and his disciples, and they stayed there for a few days.

Jesus Cleanses the Temple

[13]The Passover of the Jews was at hand, and Jesus went up to Jerusalem. [14]In the temple he found those who were selling oxen and sheep and pigeons, and the money-changers sitting there. [15]And making a whip of cords, he drove them all out of the temple, with the sheep and oxen. And he poured out the coins of the moneychangers and overturned their tables. [16]And he told those who sold the pigeons, "Take these things away; do not make my Father's house a house of trade." [17]His disciples remembered that it was written, "Zeal for your house will consume me."

[18]So the Jews said to him, "What sign do you show us for doing these things?" [19]Jesus answered them, "Destroy this temple, and in three days I will raise it up." [20]The Jews then said, "It has taken forty-six years to build this temple, and will you raise it up in three days?" [21]But he was speaking about the temple of his body. [22]When therefore he was raised from the dead, his disciples remembered that he had said this, and they believed the Scripture and the word that Jesus had spoken.

Key Verse

When therefore he was raised from the dead, his disciples remembered that he had said this, and they believed the Scripture and the word that Jesus had spoken (John 2:22).

Jesus Knows What Is in Man

[23]Now when he was in Jerusalem at the Passover Feast, many believed in his name when they saw the signs that he was doing. [24]But Jesus on his part did not entrust himself to them, because he knew all people [25]and needed no one to bear witness about man, for he himself knew what was in man.

Go Deeper

Neither the Jewish leaders nor Jesus' disciples understood His reference to "this temple" (John 2:19) as a prophecy about His death and Resurrection. Eventually the disciples saw the connection. And they even applied it in their own lives. They realized that if we receive Jesus, then we become a "space" we could call a temple. They saw that God had filled places in the past, but He wasn't confined to tabernacles or temples, nor did He live there.

In Acts 17:24, Paul takes it as a starting point that "the God who made the world and everything in it, being Lord of heaven and earth, does not live in temples made by man." Twice in 1 Corinthians (3:16 and 6:19) Paul reminds his readers that they are "God's temple." And Peter, who witnessed the events in the temple, wrote, "As you come to him, a living stone rejected by men but in the sight of God chosen and precious, you yourselves like living stones are being built up as a spiritual house, to be a holy priesthood, to offer spiritual sacrifices acceptable to God through Jesus Christ" (1 Pet. 2:4–5). What kind of shape are you in as God's temple?

eard from outside, the noises of shoppers and partygoers sound similar. Both settings usually include a musical background, loud human interaction and all the little noises people make when they are eating, bartering, drinking and doing business—the business of celebrating or the business of commerce. These were settings Jesus visited. These were settings Jesus altered by His presence.

Jesus performed His first miracle (sign) in Cana of Galilee at a wedding. In those days, weddings were community events. The whole town showed up. The rules of hospitality made the event a costly one for the families of the bride and groom. Weddings lasted days! And running out of food or drink was considered a public humiliation.

The fact that Jesus was invited to the wedding though He was not from Cana has led scholars to believe there may have been a family connection with the couple. Mary's intervention also indicates a special interest. If part of the family was disgraced, the shame might spill over to other relatives.

Mary and Jesus' brief conversation offers us a glimpse into the relationship between the Lord and His mother. She didn't tell Him what to do, but it certainly seems clear that she asked Him to do something. He reminded her in a respectful way that He was not operating on His own timetable. His actions would be in rhythm with His Heavenly Father's timing.

Mary accepted Jesus' answer and retreated. But she told the servants to "do whatever he tells you" (John 2:5). In response to her faith, Jesus transformed the stone jars full of water into the finest wine. He instantly changed what would have been an embarrassing memory into a miraculously memorable occasion!

Days later, when He arrived in Jerusalem, Jesus found the Court of the Gentiles taken over by a market. The space for silence and worship had been filled with the sounds of bleating, lowing, cooing, shouting and haggling. The Jewish temple leaders rationalized the market by claiming it was a service to pilgrims. They were not allowed to use Roman money in the offering plates, so the moneychangers made a handsome profit from providing "temple shekels." And why endure the inconvenience and difficulty of bringing a sacrificial dove or lamb to the temple when one could be bought within footsteps of the altar? For all its stench and noise, the market was a model of efficiency.

But Jesus wasn't convinced by the entrepreneurship of the merchants or the convenience of their wares. Instead He saw an affront to God and an offense to humans. God was being robbed of honor, and Gentiles were being robbed of a place to worship. Jesus took decisive action. He cleared out His Father's house.

The moneychangers and merchants fled, but the religious leaders who were also profiting from the vendors' presence demanded to know by what authority Jesus was acting: "What sign do you show us for doing these things?" (2:18). The Jewish leaders were proud of the temple (v. 20), but they were not treating it as God's house of prayer. Nor did they recognize God's presence as He walked in flesh among them.

In both situations Jesus restored order. He allowed the wedding party to continue but broke up the shopping party. The first

" *Jesus will make the joyous times unexpectedly better. But He may also intervene with what feels like violence in those areas of life where we allow the clutter of living to drown out God's whispers.* *"*

was pleasing to God; the second (transforming part of the temple into a livestock and money exchange) was deeply offensive to God. In each case, Jesus took appropriate action. He livened up the party and cleaned up the temple. He restored both places to their rightful purpose.

When we receive Jesus into our lives, He is actually present. He sees, hears and responds. We can expect the same variety of actions in our lives that we witness in this chapter. Jesus will make the joyous times unexpectedly better. But He may also intervene with what feels like violence in those areas of life where we allow the clutter of living to drown out God's whispers. Whatever the place or occasion in our lives, we don't want to miss the benefits of Jesus' presence.

Express It

Before you pray, think about those things that may have become "a cluttered marketplace" in your life. Do your desires and the constant messages of advertisers crowd your moments with God? Set aside some time, and ask Jesus to cleanse your inner place of worship from those things (good and bad) that interfere with your capacity to hear Him and speak to Him.

Consider It

As you read John 2:1–25, consider these questions:

1) What hints of a healthy relationship do you see in Jesus and Mary's exchange?

    _____

    _____

    _____

2) How well did the servants carry out Mary's request for them to "do whatever he tells you"?

    _____

    _____

    _____

3) What would cause Jesus to make "the best wine" rather than "more of the same" for the wedding party?

    _____

    _____

    _____

4) What might Jesus have meant by "My hour has not yet come" (2:4)?

    _____

    _____

    _____

5) What did locating the market in the temple's Court of the Gentiles say about the Jewish leaders' attitude toward outsiders?

    _____

    _____

    _____

6) How do Jesus' statements in this chapter illustrate His awareness of the cross?

    _____

    _____

    _____

7) Why would Jesus' understanding of people (2:24–25) cause Him to "not entrust himself to them"?

    _____

    _____

    _____

How Deep Is God's Love?

More than ever, love requires a context. The word is overused, and what it describes is undervalued. In today's world, God's love means little unless it is illustrated and visible. As we see in this lesson, God's love is a "show and tell" love.

John 3:1–36

You Must Be Born Again

3 Now there was a man of the Pharisees named Nicodemus, a ruler of the Jews. [2]This man came to Jesus by night and said to him, "Rabbi, we know that you are a teacher come from God, for no one can do these signs that you do unless God is with him." [3]Jesus answered him, "Truly, truly, I say to you, unless one is born again he cannot see the kingdom of God." [4]Nicodemus said to him, "How can a man be born when he is old? Can he enter a second time into his mother's womb and be born?" [5]Jesus answered, "Truly, truly, I say to you, unless one is born of water and the Spirit, he cannot enter the kingdom of God. [6]That which is born of the flesh is flesh, and that which is born of the Spirit is spirit. [7]Do not marvel that I said to you, 'You must be born again.' [8]The wind blows where it wishes, and you hear its sound, but you do not know where it comes from or where it goes. So it is with everyone who is born of the Spirit."

[9]Nicodemus said to him, "How can these things be?" [10]Jesus answered him, "Are you the teacher of Israel and yet you do not understand these things? [11]Truly, truly, I say to you, we speak of what we know, and bear witness to what we have seen, but you do not receive our testimony. [12]If I have told you earthly things and you do not believe, how can you believe if I tell you heavenly things? [13]No one has ascended into heaven except he who descended from heaven, the Son of Man. [14]And as Moses lifted up the serpent in the wilderness, so must the Son of Man be lifted up, [15]that whoever believes in him may have eternal life.

For God So Loved the World

[16]"For God so loved the world, that he gave his only Son, that whoever believes in him should not perish but have eternal life. [17]For God did not send his Son into the world to condemn the world, but in order that the world might be saved through him. [18]Whoever believes in him is not condemned, but whoever does not believe is condemned already, because he has not believed in the name of the only Son of God. [19]And this is the judgment: the light has come into the world, and people loved the darkness rather than the light because their deeds were evil. [20]For everyone who does wicked things hates the light and does not come to the light, lest his deeds should be exposed. [21]But whoever does what is true comes to the light, so that it may be clearly seen that his deeds have been carried out in God."

Key Verse

"For God so loved the world, that he gave his only Son, that whoever believes in him should not perish but have eternal life" (John 3:16).

John the Baptist Exalts Christ

[22]After this Jesus and his disciples went into the Judean countryside, and he remained there with them and was baptizing. [23]John also was baptizing at Aenon near Salim, because water was plentiful there, and people were coming and being baptized [24](for John had not yet been put in prison).

[25]Now a discussion arose between some of John's disciples and a Jew over purification. [26]And they came to John and said to

him, "Rabbi, he who was with you across the Jordan, to whom you bore witness—look, he is baptizing, and all are going to him." [27]John answered, "A person cannot receive even one thing unless it is given him from heaven. [28]You yourselves bear me witness, that I said, 'I am not the Christ, but I have been sent before him.' [29]The one who has the bride is the bridegroom. The friend of the bridegroom, who stands and hears him, rejoices greatly at the bridegroom's voice. Therefore this joy of mine is now complete. [30]He must increase, but I must decrease."

[31]He who comes from above is above all. He who is of the earth belongs to the earth and speaks in an earthly way. He who comes from heaven is above all. [32]He bears witness to what he has seen and heard, yet no one receives his testimony. [33]Whoever receives his testimony sets his seal to this, that God is true. [34]For he whom God has sent utters the words of God, for he gives the Spirit without measure. [35]The Father loves the Son and has given all things into his hand. [36]Whoever believes in the Son has eternal life; whoever does not obey the Son shall not see life, but the wrath of God remains on him.

Go Deeper

When Nicodemus approached Jesus, he described Jesus' miracles as "signs" (John 3:2). This word in the singular (2:18; 4:54; 6:14,30; 10:41; 12:18) and plural (2:11,23; 3:2; 4:48; 6:2,26; 7:31; 9:16; 11:47; 12:37; 20:30) has a special use in John's Gospel. Clearly, sometimes Jesus did signs or miracles, and sometimes He refused. Those who asked Him to prove Himself by doing signs usually went away unhappy. Jesus didn't do miracles on command. But if Jesus didn't do miracles to prove Who He was, then why did He do them at all?

Jesus didn't do miracles to prove He is God; He did miracles because He is God. Those who demanded signs were trying to "tempt" Jesus to display uncertainty the same way Satan tried to tempt Jesus in the wilderness. "If you are the Son of God," Satan whispered (Matt. 4:3,6). If Jesus had any doubts about His identity, He might have given into the temptation. He didn't because He never felt compelled to prove what He knew was true about Himself. If what Jesus has already done isn't proof enough for us, nothing will be proof enough.

A soft knock and a whispered exchange in the darkness interrupted the evening. The disciple who answered the door returned with an unexpected guest. Some of the disciples probably recognized Nicodemus instantly. We know that John had some connections with the Sanhedrin (John 18:15–18). Those who couldn't identify the stranger would have known from his outfit that someone of significance was seeking an audience with Jesus. Even though the conversation between Jesus and Nicodemus is often pictured as a private interview, this chapter doesn't say so. The disciples may have been a silent audience. John certainly wrote as if he was an "ear-witness" to what was said.

Nicodemus began with a compliment rather than a question: "Rabbi, we know that you are a teacher come from God, for no one can do these signs that you do unless God is with him" (3:2). This was one highly regarded religious leader telling another that he could see God was "with" Jesus.

But Jesus answered Nicodemus as if he had asked a question. The last verse of chapter 2 informed us that Jesus "knew what was in man" (v. 25). He read Nicodemus like a book. He addressed the question that was on Nicodemus' mind. What was that question? Jesus was already publicly preaching a message that echoed that of John the Baptist. Matthew 4:17 tells us that right after the temptation in the wilderness, "From that time Jesus began to preach, saying, 'Repent, for the kingdom of heaven is at hand.'"

Now, the disciples really didn't understand the nature of the kingdom. They assumed right up until the time Jesus was arrested and crucified that He was going to set up an earthly kingdom. So, we can't blame Nicodemus for the same mistake. He wanted to know under what conditions a person could become part of the kingdom Jesus was about to establish. Jesus answered him in a way he never expected: "Truly, truly, I say to you, unless one is born again he cannot see the kingdom of God" (John 3:3).

Nicodemus heard "born" with the same mind that he heard "kingdom." He didn't hear either of the terms as spiritual words. So, Jesus rephrased His statement: "Truly, truly, I say to you, unless one is born of water and the Spirit, he cannot enter the kingdom of God" (3:5). Since He said the same thing two ways, we can see that for Jesus "born again" equals "born of water and Spirit" (or twice born—physical and spiritual) and that "see the kingdom of God" means "enter the kingdom of God."

Nicodemus, still confused, asked Jesus, "How can these things be?" (v. 9). He had trouble understanding what Jesus was telling him about earthly and heavenly things. But there is a difference between understanding and believing. Understanding is never the requirement for salvation; faith is. Jesus answered Nicodemus' confusion with an invitation to believe.

The concept of being born again is as foreign today as it was to Nicodemus. But we have already seen this picture here in John. John 1:13 introduced the spiritual rebirth. All who receive Jesus, who believe in His name, get to be children of God, "who were born, not of blood nor of the will of the flesh nor of the will of man, but of God" (1:13). Acknowledging and believing in Jesus is part of a spiritual rebirth process in which God brings a new life into His kingdom. That new life is an eternal life. It's not a process we can do by our wills but something God is willing to do for us. Yet, like Nicodemus, people today shake their heads and say, "How can these things be?"

If you're looking for a complicated answer, you'll miss the clear answer Jesus gave. How can these things be? Because of God's love for us—a love so great that it would send Jesus as the living, dying and living again guarantee of that love (Rom. 5:8). John 3:16 doesn't tell us, "that whoever understands" or "that whoever figures it out" receives eternal life. The effective response to God's gift of Jesus is "that whoever *believes in him* should not perish but have eternal life" (emphasis added).

Meeting Jesus is a central theme of the Gospel of John. But meeting Jesus is a lot like meeting anyone. An introduction and

> *" Jesus won't settle for being among our acquaintances. That's not why He came. He came to provide eternal life to all who go beyond meeting Him to believing in Him. "*

handshake doesn't mean that we trust our new acquaintance. And Jesus won't settle for being among our acquaintances. That's not why He came. He came to provide eternal life to all who go beyond meeting Him to believing in Him. Don't forget John's purpose in writing his Gospel: "These are written so that you may believe that Jesus is the Christ, the Son of God, and that by believing you may have life in his name" (20:31).

Express It

Substitute all the words in John 3:16 that begin with "w" with your own name, and then turn that verse into a personal prayer. Tell Jesus what it means to you to believe in Him. And if this is the first time you've ever prayed a prayer like that, realize that you have just received God's gift of eternal life.

Consider It

As you read John 3:1–36, consider these questions:

1) Why would someone like Nicodemus come to Jesus at night?

_____

_____

_____

2) At what point do you think that insisting on a better understanding becomes an excuse for refusing to believe?

_____

_____

_____

3) Verses 17–21 provide the alternative results if we decide not to believe in Jesus. Why is this an important part of the message?

_____

_____

_____

4) How would you describe your present relationship with Jesus?

_____

_____

_____

5) What do you learn about Jesus from John the Baptist in verses 22–36?

_____

_____

_____

6) What do you learn about John the Baptist in those verses?

_____

_____

_____

7) How do your statements about Jesus parallel John's?

_____

_____

_____

Meeting Jesus at the Water Cooler

You can find out a lot about people by observing them in conversation. Who speaks first? How do they treat others? Do they listen? And what do they talk about? In this lesson, we listen in as Jesus speaks to a woman who was used to being ignored and insulted. What happened when she met Christ?

John 4:1–54

Jesus and the Woman of Samaria

4 Now when Jesus learned that the Pharisees had heard that Jesus was making and baptizing more disciples than John ² (although Jesus himself did not baptize, but only his disciples), ³he left Judea and departed again for Galilee. ⁴And he had to pass through Samaria. ⁵So he came to a town of Samaria called Sychar, near the field that Jacob had given to his son Joseph. ⁶Jacob's well was there; so Jesus, wearied as he was from his journey, was sitting beside the well. It was about the sixth hour.

⁷There came a woman of Samaria to draw water. Jesus said to her, "Give me a drink." ⁸(For his disciples had gone away into the city to buy food.) ⁹The Samaritan woman said to him, "How is it that you, a Jew, ask for a drink from me, a woman of Samaria?" (For Jews have no dealings with Samaritans.) ¹⁰Jesus answered her, "If you knew the gift of God, and who it is that is saying to you, 'Give me a drink,' you would have asked him, and he would have given you living water." ¹¹The woman said to him, "Sir, you have nothing to draw water with, and the well is deep. Where do you get that living water? ¹²Are you greater than our father Jacob? He gave us the well and drank from it himself, as did his sons and his livestock." ¹³Jesus said to her, "Everyone who drinks of this water will be thirsty again, ¹⁴but whoever drinks of the water that I will give him will never be thirsty forever. The water that I will give him will become in him a spring of water welling up to eternal life." ¹⁵The woman said to him, "Sir, give me this water, so that I will not be thirsty or have to come here to draw water."

¹⁶Jesus said to her, "Go, call your husband, and come here." ¹⁷The woman answered him, "I have no husband." Jesus said to her, "You are right in saying, 'I have no husband'; ¹⁸for you have had five husbands, and the one you now have is not your husband. What you have said is true." ¹⁹The woman said to him, "Sir, I perceive that you are a prophet. ²⁰Our fathers worshiped on this mountain, but you say that in Jerusalem is the place where people ought to worship." ²¹Jesus said to her, "Woman, believe me, the hour is coming when neither on this mountain nor in Jerusalem will you worship the Father. ²²You worship what you do not know; we worship what we know, for salvation is from the Jews. ²³But the hour is coming, and is now here, when the true worshipers will worship the Father in spirit and truth, for the Father is seeking such people to worship him. ²⁴God is spirit, and those who worship him must worship in spirit and truth." ²⁵The woman said to him, "I know that Messiah is coming (he who is called Christ). When he comes, he will tell us all things." ²⁶Jesus said to her, "I who speak to you am he."

²⁷Just then his disciples came back. They marveled that he was talking with a woman, but no one said, "What do you seek?" or, "Why are you talking with her?" ²⁸So the woman left her water jar and went away into town and said to the people, ²⁹"Come, see a man who told me all that I ever did. Can this be the Christ?" ³⁰They went out of the town and were coming to him.

³¹Meanwhile the disciples were urging him, saying, "Rabbi, eat." ³²But he said to them, "I have food to eat that you do not know about." ³³So the disciples said to one another, "Has anyone brought him something to eat?" ³⁴Jesus said to them, "My food is to do the will of him who sent me and to accomplish his work. ³⁵Do you not say, 'There are yet four months, then comes the harvest'? Look, I tell you, lift up your eyes, and see that the fields are white

for harvest. ³⁶Already the one who reaps is receiving wages and gathering fruit for eternal life, so that sower and reaper may rejoice together. ³⁷For here the saying holds true, 'One sows and another reaps.' ³⁸I sent you to reap that for which you did not labor. Others have labored, and you have entered into their labor."

Key Verse

They said to the woman, "It is no longer because of what you said that we believe, for we have heard for ourselves, and we know that this is indeed the Savior of the world" (John 4:42).

³⁹Many Samaritans from that town believed in him because of the woman's testimony, "He told me all that I ever did." ⁴⁰So when the Samaritans came to him, they asked him to stay with them, and he stayed there two days. ⁴¹And many more believed because of his word. ⁴²They said to the woman, "It is no longer because of what you said that we believe, for we have heard for ourselves, and we know that this is indeed the Savior of the world."

⁴³After the two days he departed for Galilee. ⁴⁴(For Jesus himself had testified that a prophet has no honor in his own hometown.) ⁴⁵So when he came to Galilee, the Galileans welcomed him, having seen all that he had done in Jerusalem at the feast. For they too had gone to the feast.

Jesus Heals an Official's Son

⁴⁶So he came again to Cana in Galilee, where he had made the water wine. And at Capernaum there was an official whose son was ill. ⁴⁷When this man heard that Jesus had come from Judea to Galilee, he went to him and asked him to come down and heal his son, for he was at the point of death. ⁴⁸So Jesus said to him, "Unless you see signs and wonders you will not believe." ⁴⁹The official said to him, "Sir, come down before my child dies." ⁵⁰Jesus said to him, "Go; your son will live." The man believed the word that Jesus spoke to him and went on his way. ⁵¹As he was going down, his servants met him and told him that his son was recovering. ⁵²So he asked them the hour when he began to get better, and they said to him, "Yesterday at the seventh hour the fever left him." ⁵³The father knew that was the hour when Jesus had said to him, "Your son will live." And he himself believed, and all his household. ⁵⁴This was now the second sign that Jesus did when he had come from Judea to Galilee.

Go Deeper

People often explain their reluctance to share their faith by saying, "Well, I just don't know what to tell people. And what if they ask me a question I can't answer?" What do you think your friends (or strangers) would say if you began a conversation with, "Come, see a man who told me all that I ever did. Can this be the Christ?" (John 4:29).

The woman at the well shared her experience and invited people to check

(continued)

Go Deeper Continued ...

out Jesus for themselves. That's a beautiful way to start. You don't have to know all the answers. But you do have to identify and express what Jesus has done for you. Put that clearly and honestly into words, and you will be amazed at the way people respond to Jesus. When did you last have a conversation with someone about Jesus? When will you have your next one?

She approached the well cautiously. Long past worrying about dignity, she just wanted a little privacy. So, she came at high noon, with the heat beating down, anxious to fetch her water and hurry home. The pottery jar already digging into her shoulder, once filled with water, would be agony under the sun. Then she saw the stranger, sitting by the well. *So much for privacy*, she thought.

When she got closer, she noticed he was a Jew. As a Samaritan (and a woman), she expected to be deliberately ignored. *At least I won't have to talk to him*, she thought. *Maybe I can get this over with quickly.*

She was about to lower her jar into the well when he spoke, startling her.

"Give me a drink." It wasn't an order with a disdainful tone but a calm request from one thirsty human being to another.

She was amazed. He had just broken several unwritten ironclad rules. Jewish men didn't speak to women they didn't know. Jews kept their distance from Samaritans. And they certainly didn't ask Samaritans for a drink. Jesus' casual and open expression provoked an honest response from her. "You're a Jew; I'm a Samaritan. Should we be having this conversation? I can't believe you're asking me for a drink."

His next words made her forget her earlier curiosity because they gave her a new puzzle to think about. "Actually," Jesus said, "if you knew who I am, you'd be asking me for water. I can give you the living kind." (See John 4:10.)

Now the woman was both amused and amazed. *How can this empty-handed man be offering me water? Where's he going to get it? Why did he mention God and call his water "living"?* She put these thoughts into words and then pointed out to this stranger that he was in danger of claiming to be somehow greater than ancient Jacob whose well they seemed to be discussing.

Once again Jesus caught her attention with His answer. "Everyone who drinks of this water [Jacob's well] will be thirsty again, but whoever drinks of the water that I will give him will never be thirsty forever. The water that I will give him will become in him a spring of water welling up to eternal life" (4:13–14).

As He spoke, the woman became aware of the deep thirst in her life. She realized it would be wonderful to have living water—especially if it meant she would never have to come to this well again! Their roles became completely reversed when the woman who had moments before been asked by Jesus for a drink now found herself asking Him for living water.

But Jesus wasn't done surprising her. He shifted the discussion from thirst quenching to life quenching when He asked her to get her husband. She answered with as much truth as she dared at the moment. "I have no husband" (v.17).

Jesus affirmed her even as He pointed out she was not telling the whole truth (vv. 17–18). She had five husbands before the man she was living with now.

The woman tried to counter Jesus' awareness with an observation of her own: "I perceive that you are a prophet" (v. 19). She wanted to shift the discussion away from the moral chaos in her life to a safer subject—religion. *Perhaps*, she thought, *since he's tolerated me as a woman and a Samaritan, maybe he will be tolerant in religion.* So, she expressed an "each of us has our own religion" kind of comment.

Rather than responding with an argument, Jesus gave her an answer. Worshiping God isn't about location or cultural background—it's about truth and Spirit.

> " *Worshiping God isn't about location or cultural background—it's about truth and Spirit.* "

No one had ever spoken to her or understood her the way this man had just demonstrated. She couldn't imagine anyone being greater except one, the expected Savior she had heard about all her life. She told Jesus her deepest hope—that she would be able to understand when the Messiah came because "he will tell us all things" (v. 25).

Jesus informed her, "I who speak to you am he" (v. 26).

What a powerful mixture of hope and faith must have filled her! Though she had come to the well at noon to avoid public contact, she now rushed back into the village to tell everyone about the man who might be the Messiah. Her message created a stir. Many were touched by her transformation, and all came to hear Jesus. He stayed for two days and left a town changed.

The conversations we have at the water cooler, coffee machine or lounge can be used by God to transform people's lives. People meet Jesus in unusual places all the time. Those who follow Him need to remember and let others know that He's with them wherever they go.

Express It

Think about several people in your life who have probably never met Jesus. As you pray, tell God you're available to introduce them to Him. Talk to God about what you would say to each of those people about Him. If you're used to praying silently, do this exercise out loud. Get used to hearing your voice talk about Jesus. Nothing pleases our Heavenly Father more than to hear us talk about His Son!

Consider It

As you read John 4:1–54, consider these questions:

1) Why did Jesus stop in Sychar? What does that reason tell you about Him?

2) Describe the role of the disciples here and what Jesus taught them.

3) What crucial points was Jesus making in verses 21–24?

4) Explain what the townspeople told the woman in verse 42.

5) John 4:46–54 records a second miracle (sign) in Cana. How was this one different from the first miracle (2:1–11)?

6) What are the limits of miracles in bringing people to faith? Do they always work?

7) What were the conversational and miraculous turning points that led you to recognize Jesus Christ as Lord and Savior?

How to Use a Sabbath

The same Jesus who got serious about the way people used the temple seemed to take a very casual approach about using the Sabbath. His culture had piles of rules about how to live on "God's seventh day," but Jesus seemed ready to walk all over them. What was He doing?

John 5:1–47

The Healing at the Pool on the Sabbath

5 After this there was a feast of the Jews, and Jesus went up to Jerusalem.

²Now there is in Jerusalem by the Sheep Gate a pool, in Aramaic called Bethesda, which has five roofed colonnades. ³In these lay a multitude of invalids—blind, lame, and paralyzed. ⁵One man was there who had been an invalid for thirty-eight years. ⁶When Jesus saw him lying there and knew that he had already been there a long time, he said to him, "Do you want to be healed?" ⁷The sick man answered him, "Sir, I have no one to put me into the pool when the water is stirred up, and while I am going another steps down before me." ⁸Jesus said to him, "Get up, take up your bed, and walk." ⁹And at once the man was healed, and he took up his bed and walked.

> # Key Verse
>
> *But Jesus answered them, "My Father is working until now, and I am working"* (John 5:17).

Now that day was the Sabbath. ¹⁰So the Jews said to the man who had been healed, "It is the Sabbath, and it is not lawful for you to take up your bed." ¹¹But he answered them, "The man who healed me, that man said to me, 'Take up your bed, and walk.'" ¹²They asked him, "Who is the man who said to you, 'Take up your bed and walk'?" ¹³Now the man who had been healed did not know who it was, for Jesus had withdrawn, as there was a crowd in the place. ¹⁴Afterward Jesus found him in the temple and said to him, "See, you are well! Sin no more, that nothing worse may happen to you." ¹⁵The man went away and told the Jews that it was Jesus who had healed him. ¹⁶And this was why the Jews were persecuting Jesus, because he was doing these things on the Sabbath. ¹⁷But Jesus answered them, "My Father is working until now, and I am working."

Jesus Is Equal with God

¹⁸This was why the Jews were seeking all the more to kill him, because not only was he breaking the Sabbath, but he was even calling God his own Father, making himself equal with God.

The Authority of the Son

¹⁹So Jesus said to them, "Truly, truly, I say to you, the Son can do nothing of his own accord, but only what he sees the Father doing. For whatever the Father does, that the Son does likewise. ²⁰For the Father loves the Son and shows him all that he himself is doing. And greater works than these will he show him, so that you may marvel. ²¹For as the Father raises the dead and gives them life, so also the Son gives life to whom he will. ²²The Father judges no one, but has given all judgment to the Son, ²³that all may honor the Son, just as they honor the Father. Whoever does not honor the Son does not honor the Father who sent him. ²⁴Truly, truly, I say to you, whoever hears my word and believes him who sent me has eternal life. He does not come into judgment, but has passed from death to life.

²⁵"Truly, truly, I say to you, an hour is coming, and is now here, when the dead will hear the voice of the Son of God, and those who hear will live. ²⁶For as the Father has life in himself, so he has granted the Son also to have life in himself. ²⁷And he

has given him authority to execute judgment, because he is the Son of Man. ²⁸Do not marvel at this, for an hour is coming when all who are in the tombs will hear his voice ²⁹and come out, those who have done good to the resurrection of life, and those who have done evil to the resurrection of judgment.

Witnesses to Jesus

³⁰"I can do nothing on my own. As I hear, I judge, and my judgment is just, because I seek not my own will but the will of him who sent me. ³¹If I alone bear witness about myself, my testimony is not deemed true. ³²There is another who bears witness about me, and I know that the testimony that he bears about me is true. ³³You sent to John, and he has borne witness to the truth. ³⁴Not that the testimony that I receive is from man, but I say these things so that you may be saved. ³⁵He was a burning and shining lamp, and you were willing to rejoice for a while in his light. ³⁶But the testimony that I have is greater than that of John. For the works that the Father has given me to accomplish, the very works that I am doing, bear witness about me that the Father has sent me. ³⁷And the Father who sent me has himself borne witness about me. His voice you have never heard, his form you have never seen, ³⁸and you do not have his word abiding in you, for you do not believe the one whom he has sent. ³⁹You search the Scriptures because you think that in them you have eternal life; and it is they that bear witness about me, ⁴⁰yet you refuse to come to me that you may have life. ⁴¹I do not receive glory from people. ⁴²But I know that you do not have the love of God within you. ⁴³I have come in my Father's name, and you do not receive me. If another comes in his own name, you will receive him. ⁴⁴How can you believe, when you receive glory from one another and do not seek the glory that comes from the only God? ⁴⁵Do not think that I will accuse you to the Father. There is one who accuses you: Moses, on whom you have set your hope. ⁴⁶If you believed Moses, you would believe me; for he wrote of me. ⁴⁷But if you do not believe his writings, how will you believe my words?"

Go Deeper

Jesus had five Sabbath showdowns (John 5:1–18; Mark 3:1–6; Luke 13:10–17; 14:1–6; John 9:1–16). He got into a lot of trouble over the Sabbath. When Jesus said, "The Sabbath was made for man, not man for the Sabbath" (Mark 2:27), He was pointing out that the best way to "rest" (the meaning of Sabbath) is to find something that renews us for serving God in our work. When the psalmist wrote, "This is the day that the LORD has made; let us rejoice and be glad in it" (Ps. 118:24), he wasn't just speaking about the Sabbath. He was speaking about every day.

The Old Testament makes it clear that God established the Sabbath as a recurring "sign" day for His chosen people (Ex. 20:8–11; 31:12–17; Ezek. 20:12). But Jesus fulfilled the Law—part of what He meant when He said "It is finished" (John 19:30). Sunday isn't a Christian Sabbath—it's the day we remember the Resurrection of Jesus. It's not a day to rest but a day to rejoice!

There is wisdom in a healthy cycle of work and rest, but Christians are free to live each and every day for Christ. (See Col. 3:17.)

Y ou may remember the inspiring film *Chariots of Fire*. The movie tells part of the story of Eric Liddell, the son of Scottish missionaries in China. He returned to England for school and became one of the heroes of the 1924 Olympics. He later went to China himself and was confined and died in a Japanese P.O.W. camp during World War II.

But Eric's moment of fame during the Olympics was threatened when they scheduled his qualifying heats on Sunday. He refused to run on the Lord's Day. He was a favorite to win but passed up an opportunity for glory. Instead, he spent the day sharing his faith and worshiping with other believers. But ultimately his steadfast convictions brought even more glory to God. One of his teammates yielded his place in another race that Eric won, and he still made a mark in the record books.

Jesus and the Jews who hounded Him all based their approach to the Sabbath (what we would call Saturday) on the fourth of the Ten Commandments (Ex. 20:8–11). The people in Jesus' day lived with a long list of detailed rules designed to "keep the Sabbath holy." These rules covered how many steps you could take, places you could go, items you could eat, actions you could perform—all intended to keep people from "working" on the Sabbath. But is that the reason for the Sabbath? And did Jesus' handling of Sabbath issues point us to God's ultimate purpose in fulfilling the Law (the commandments) and setting us free to live for God each and every day?

We who live after Jesus' death and Resurrection must never forget that He does for us what we could never do for ourselves— bring us into right relationship with God. The commandments of God, which were intended to highlight each person's need for God's grace, had become, by Jesus' day, an endless drudgery of rule-keeping. The Sabbath commandment was an especially "tempting" one because it appeared so "do-able." The problem is, once a person decides to earn God's favor by rule-keeping rather than surrendering to God's grace, then the whole Law applies. (See James 2:10.)

One sunny Sabbath day, Jesus strolled beside the healing pool by the Sheep Gate and approached a man who had been stuck on a mat for 38 years. When Jesus healed this man and instructed him to carry away his mat, His directions involved the man in Sabbath-breaking. Those who accosted the man and demanded an explanation didn't seem to be at all impressed that the man could suddenly walk—their whole attention was focused on the bedroll under his arm. The man, taken by surprise, could only shrug his shoulders and say, "Hey, the man who healed me told me to take up my bed and walk. How could I refuse?" After the hubbub died down, Jesus sought out the man to warn him his new freedom didn't exempt him from sin.

When the healed man identified Jesus to the authorities, they began to harass Him. They instinctively distrusted and feared someone who did on the Sabbath, and every day, what they couldn't do even on their best day. Jesus' words to His persecutors deserve our attention: "My Father is working until now, and I am working" (John 5:17).

In this brief statement, Jesus answered their accusation and affirmed His own divinity. The Jews of Jesus' day did not usually call God, "Father." That was too familiar. Yet Jesus not only used the term but also later explained it as the best description of their shared identity—"I and the Father are one" (10:30). Father and Son may have rested from Creation, but They were ever at work bringing about salvation to the world.

Which brings us back to today and our understanding of the Sabbath. First, followers of Jesus should not confuse the Sabbath with the Lord's Day (see *Go Deeper*). The early Christians kept both days, but by the end of the New Testament, the Lord's Day was the priority as a day of worship and fellowship.

> ❝ *Our focus on the Lord's Day should not be on how to avoid any appearance of work, but on how to honor and love God by practicing compassion toward those around us.* ❞

Believers should also not forget that Jesus never equated "rest" with eating a huge meal and then spending an afternoon napping. This ought to be our purpose every day, but particularly on the Lord's Day.

Express It

As you pray, meditate on the way your perceptions of Jesus have changed over the past five years. How do you know you have come to know Him better? In what ways has knowing Jesus made a difference for you in these years? Talk to Him about those changes and about how you feel regarding His work in your life.

Consider It

As you read John 5:1–47, consider these questions:

1) How do you relate with the condition of someone who was stuck in one place for 38 years?

2) Why do you think Jesus chose to heal this man among the many others who needed healing?

3) What were the two claims Jesus made that irritated the Jewish leaders the most?

4) What are the main points about His relationship to the Father that Jesus made in this chapter?

5) How did Jesus describe the way some were misusing the Scriptures (vv. 38–40)?

6) In what ways has Jesus helped and healed the helpless places in your life?

7) What are your most basic reasons for trusting Christ?

Bread from the Baker's Maker

I love the smell of hot bread. The aroma of fresh loaves has a comforting effect. Those involved in disaster relief find that getting the bakeries up and running is one of the first signs of hope that life will go on. In many places in the world, bread represents life. In this lesson, we'll discover what Jesus meant when He called Himself the Bread of Life.

John 6:1–71

Jesus Feeds the Five Thousand

6 After this Jesus went away to the other side of the Sea of Galilee, which is the Sea of Tiberias. ²And a large crowd was following him, because they saw the signs that he was doing on the sick. ³Jesus went up on the mountain, and there he sat down with his disciples. ⁴Now the Passover, the feast of the Jews, was at hand. ⁵Lifting up his eyes, then, and seeing that a large crowd was coming toward him, Jesus said to Philip, "Where are we to buy bread, so that these people may eat?" ⁶He said this to test him, for he himself knew what he would do. ⁷Philip answered him, "Two hundred denarii would not buy enough bread for each of them to get a little." ⁸One of his disciples, Andrew, Simon Peter's brother, said to him, ⁹"There is a boy here who has five barley loaves and two fish, but what are they for so many?" ¹⁰Jesus said, "Have the people sit down." Now there was much grass in the place. So the men sat down, about five thousand in number. ¹¹Jesus then took the loaves, and when he had given thanks, he distributed them to those who were seated. So also the fish, as much as they wanted. ¹²And when they had eaten their fill, he told his disciples, "Gather up the leftover fragments, that nothing may be lost." ¹³So they gathered them up and filled twelve baskets with fragments from the five barley loaves, left by those who had eaten. ¹⁴When the people saw the sign that he had done, they said, "This is indeed the Prophet who is to come into the world!"

¹⁵Perceiving then that they were about to come and take him by force to make him king, Jesus withdrew again to the mountain by himself.

Jesus Walks on Water

¹⁶When evening came, his disciples went down to the sea, ¹⁷got into a boat, and started across the sea to Capernaum. It was now dark, and Jesus had not yet come to them. ¹⁸The sea became rough because a strong wind was blowing. ¹⁹When they had rowed about three or four miles, they saw Jesus walking on the sea and coming near the boat, and they were frightened. ²⁰But he said to them, "It is I; do not be afraid." ²¹Then they were glad to take him into the boat, and immediately the boat was at the land to which they were going.

> # Key Verse
>
> *Jesus said to them, "I am the bread of life; whoever comes to me shall not hunger, and whoever believes in me shall never thirst"* (John 6:35).

I Am the Bread of Life

²²On the next day the crowd that remained on the other side of the sea saw that there had been only one boat there, and that Jesus had not entered the boat with his disciples, but that his disciples had gone away alone. ²³Other boats from Tiberias came near the place where they had eaten the bread after the Lord had given thanks. ²⁴So when the crowd saw that Jesus was not there, nor his disciples, they themselves got into the boats and went to Capernaum, seeking Jesus.

²⁵When they found him on the other side of the sea, they said to him, "Rabbi, when did you come here?" ²⁶Jesus

answered them, "Truly, truly, I say to you, you are seeking me, not because you saw signs, but because you ate your fill of the loaves. 27Do not labor for the food that perishes, but for the food that endures to eternal life, which the Son of Man will give to you. For on him God the Father has set his seal." 28Then they said to him, "What must we do, to be doing the works of God?" 29Jesus answered them, "This is the work of God, that you believe in him whom he has sent." 30So they said to him, "Then what sign do you do, that we may see and believe you? What work do you perform? 31Our fathers ate the manna in the wilderness; as it is written, 'He gave them bread from heaven to eat.'" 32Jesus then said to them, "Truly, truly, I say to you, it was not Moses who gave you the bread from heaven, but my Father gives you the true bread from heaven. 33For the bread of God is he who comes down from heaven and gives life to the world." 34They said to him, "Sir, give us this bread always."

35Jesus said to them, "I am the bread of life; whoever comes to me shall not hunger, and whoever believes in me shall never thirst. 36But I said to you that you have seen me and yet do not believe. 37All that the Father gives me will come to me, and whoever comes to me I will never cast out. 38For I have come down from heaven, not to do my own will but the will of him who sent me. 39And this is the will of him who sent me, that I should lose nothing of all that he has given me, but raise it up on the last day. 40For this is the will of my Father, that everyone who looks on the Son and believes in him should have eternal life, and I will raise him up on the last day."

41So the Jews grumbled about him, because he said, "I am the bread that came down from heaven." 42They said, "Is not this Jesus, the son of Joseph, whose father and mother we know? How does he now say, 'I have come down from heaven'?" 43Jesus answered them, "Do not grumble among yourselves. 44No one can come to me unless the Father who sent me draws him. And I will raise him up on the last day. 45It is written in the Prophets, 'And they will all be taught by God.' Everyone who has heard and learned from the Father comes to me— 46not that anyone has seen the Father except he who is from God; he has seen the Father. 47Truly, truly, I say to you, whoever believes has eternal life. 48I am the bread of life. 49Your fathers ate the manna in the wilderness, and they died. 50This is the bread that comes down from heaven, so that one may eat of it and not die. 51I am the living bread that came down from heaven. If anyone eats of this bread, he will live forever. And the bread that I will give for the life of the world is my flesh."

52The Jews then disputed among themselves, saying, "How can this man give us his flesh to eat?" 53So Jesus said to them, "Truly, truly, I say to you, unless you eat the flesh of the Son of Man and drink his blood, you have no life in you. 54Whoever feeds on my flesh and drinks my blood has eternal life, and I will raise him up on the last day. 55For my flesh is true food, and my blood is true drink. 56Whoever feeds on my flesh and drinks my blood abides in me, and I in him. 57As the living Father sent me, and I live because of the Father, so whoever feeds on me, he also will live because of me. 58This is the bread that came down from heaven, not as the fathers ate and died. Whoever feeds on this bread will live forever." 59Jesus said these things in the synagogue, as he taught at Capernaum.

The Words of Eternal Life

60When many of his disciples heard it, they said, "This is a hard saying; who can listen to it?" 61But Jesus, knowing in himself that his disciples were grumbling about this, said to them, "Do you take offense at this? 62Then what if you were to see the Son of Man ascending to where he was before? 63It is the Spirit who gives life;

the flesh is of no avail. The words that I have spoken to you are spirit and life. ⁶⁴But there are some of you who do not believe." (For Jesus knew from the beginning who those were who did not believe, and who it was who would betray him.) ⁶⁵And he said, "This is why I told you that no one can come to me unless it is granted him by the Father."

⁶⁶After this many of his disciples turned back and no longer walked with him. ⁶⁷So Jesus said to the Twelve, "Do you want to go away as well?" ⁶⁸Simon Peter answered him, "Lord, to whom shall we go? You have the words of eternal life, ⁶⁹and we have believed, and have come to know, that you are the Holy One of God." ⁷⁰Jesus answered them, "Did I not choose you, the Twelve? And yet one of you is a devil." ⁷¹He spoke of Judas the son of Simon Iscariot, for he, one of the Twelve, was going to betray him.

Go Deeper

In John 6:35, Jesus announces the first of nine "I am" sayings recorded in this Gospel: "I am the bread of life." The other instances are:

- John 8:12— "I am the light of the world."
- John 8:58—"Before Abraham was, I am."
- John 9:5— "I am the light of the world."
- John 10:7,9,— "I am the door."
- John 10:11,14—"I am the good shepherd."
- John 11:25— "I am the resurrection and the life."
- John 14:6— "I am the way, and the truth, and the life."
- John 15:1,5—"I am the true vine."

The "I am" phrase had a powerful historical meaning for Israelites. It was the name God gave Himself in Exodus 3:14. Jesus used the term deliberately as part of His claim to divinity. We know this because those who heard Him reacted to the phrase (John 8:59). They *knew* what He was claiming and didn't like it.

Notice how each claim (bread, light, door, resurrection and life, way, truth, vine) points to the ways God makes Himself known to us by meeting our deepest physical *and* spiritual needs. No one else can do this for us. Jesus demonstrated by His words, life, death and Resurrection that He is "I Am."

*H*ow did He do that? The disciples had seen Jesus transform water into wine. Now they sat watching thousands enjoy a lunch of bread and fish, the result of Jesus' breaking apart five loaves and two fish. So much from so little! They went from "not nearly enough" to "lots left over"—12 baskets full of bread after all had eaten their fill.

How did He do that? After this miraculous picnic, Jesus dismissed the crowd and sent His disciples back across the lake to Capernaum while He stayed alone on the hillside. They had been rowing against the wind for some time when they saw Him strolling among the waves toward them. Now that was strange enough to be frightening. But when Jesus spoke to them, they welcomed Him into the boat, which suddenly arrived at the far shore.

How did He do that? That's what the crowd thought the next morning when they realized that Jesus had somehow left with His disciples even though they hadn't seen Him get into the boat with them. They hurried to catch up with Him.

Jesus welcomed them with the observation: "You are seeking me, not because you saw signs, but because you ate your fill of the loaves. Do not labor for the food that perishes, but for the food that endures to eternal life, which the Son of Man will give to you. For on him God the Father has set his seal" (John 6:26–27).

They thought they had found the ideal king—someone who could give them bread and fish every day. Jesus pointed out how easy it is to seek to meet Him for the wrong reasons. When we come to Jesus with our plans and agenda in hand, we may never find Him. Jesus didn't answer every question or meet every need that was presented to Him. He often took time to show the person's even deeper needs.

In the last lesson, Jesus healed a lame man but pointed out his need for help with sin. Jesus showed the woman at the well that her real thirst had to do with her soul, not her body. Even when "significant people" in Jesus' life, like His family, came with requests (Mark 3:31–35), He sometimes turned them away. His brother James must have remembered that lesson clearly, for in his own letter he wrote, "You ask and do not receive, because you ask wrongly, to spend it on your passions" (James 4:3). Unless we understand and are willing to say, "Your will be done," we will not discover what we desperately need—Jesus Himself.

As was true of the crowds chasing Jesus, our immediate needs seem crucial. We can't understand why God wouldn't see them as just as important as they seem to us. We need bread, healing, answers, jobs, friends and a thousand other pressing requests that we bring to Him. And as important as these truly are, they are not the most important.

Again, notice how the crowd reacted to Jesus' words about expanding their purposes. He said, "Do not labor for the food that perishes, but for the food that endures to eternal life, which the Son of Man will give to you" (John 6:27). They basically insisted that if He was going to be their leader, then, like Moses, He would need to provide them with daily bread (manna). Jesus reminded them that even though God had provided manna all those years in the wilderness, the people still died. That's not the kind of bread He was offering.

Still not understanding, they asked for His bread. He answered, "I am the bread." Their disappointment and anger almost oozes from the Bible page. *That* wasn't the bread they wanted. They wanted their bread, and they wanted to eat it too.

Some of the clearest moments of truth in our relationship with God come when He *doesn't* answer our prayers—at least not with what we expected. Somehow, when we ask for something and He responds by offering nothing more than Himself, we are tempted to think we're getting less rather than infinitely more than we asked for!

At this point we have a choice. We can insist that God prove He is giving us Himself by giving us what we've asked for (like the crowd did with the bread), or we can trust that He knows better what we really need and express our trust in Him.

"Some of the clearest moments of truth in our relationship with God come when He doesn't answer our prayers— at least not with what we expected. "

The choice may look easy on paper, but it often proves difficult in life. John 6:66 tells us, "After this many of his disciples turned back and no longer walked with him." It's hard when we don't get our way with God. But He loves us too much not to teach us that He knows best—even when we don't like the lesson.

Express It

As you pray, consider how you usually approach Jesus. How would you describe your attitude: casual, reverent, frightened, doubtful, hurried? How does your attitude reveal what you think of Him? Use this prayer time to clarify what you expect from the Lord when you pray. Ask Him to teach you a healthy balance between confidence and flexibility, between expectation and submission, when you present requests to Him.

Consider It

As you read John 6:1–71, consider these questions:

1) Why did Jesus ask His disciples to provide food for the crowd?

2) Who benefited most from the feeding of the 5,000–the crowd or the disciples?

3) Why didn't the people accept Jesus' claim that He is the Bread of Life?

4) According to verse 68, what did the disciples conclude was the correct answer to, "How did He do that?"

5) Why did so many of Jesus' followers decide to leave Him at this point in His ministry?

6) What reasons could Jesus have had for revealing that one of the Twelve would betray Him?

7) What does Jesus' being the Bread of Life mean to you?

Why Do So Many Hate Jesus?

The rapid escalation of hostilities against Jesus catches us by surprise. How could such a popular figure turn into a persecuted pariah? In this lesson, we'll see how Jesus challenged His listeners to make a choice about His identity—the same challenge He gives to each one of us today.

John 7:1–52

Jesus at the Feast of Booths

7 After this Jesus went about in Galilee. He would not go about in Judea, because the Jews were seeking to kill him. ²Now the Jews' Feast of Booths was at hand. ³So his brothers said to him, "Leave here and go to Judea, that your disciples also may see the works you are doing. ⁴For no one works in secret if he seeks to be known openly. If you do these things, show yourself to the world." ⁵For not even his brothers believed in him. ⁶Jesus said to them, "My time has not yet come, but your time is always here. ⁷The world cannot hate you, but it hates me because I testify about it that its works are evil. ⁸You go up to the feast. I am not going up to this feast, for my time has not yet fully come." ⁹After saying this, he remained in Galilee.

¹⁰But after his brothers had gone up to the feast, then he also went up, not publicly but in private. ¹¹The Jews were looking for him at the feast, and saying, "Where is he?" ¹²And there was much muttering about him among the people. While some said, "He is a good man," others said, "No, he is leading the people astray." ¹³Yet for fear of the Jews no one spoke openly of him.

¹⁴About the middle of the feast Jesus went up into the temple and began teaching. ¹⁵The Jews therefore marveled, saying, "How is it that this man has learning, when he has never studied?" ¹⁶So Jesus answered them, "My teaching is not mine, but his who sent me. ¹⁷If anyone's will is to do God's will, he will know whether the teaching is from God or whether I am speaking on my own authority. ¹⁸The one who speaks on his own authority seeks his own glory, but the one who seeks the glory of him who sent him is true, and in him there is no falsehood. ¹⁹Has not Moses given you the law? Yet none of you keeps the law. Why do you seek to kill me?" ²⁰The crowd answered, "You have a demon! Who is seeking to kill you?" ²¹Jesus answered them, "I did one deed, and you all marvel at it. ²²Moses gave you circumcision (not that it is from Moses, but from the fathers), and you circumcise a man on the Sabbath. ²³If on the Sabbath a man receives circumcision, so that the law of Moses may not be broken, are you angry with me because on the Sabbath I made a man's whole body well? ²⁴Do not judge by appearances, but judge with right judgment."

Can This Be the Christ?

²⁵Some of the people of Jerusalem therefore said, "Is not this the man whom they seek to kill? ²⁶And here he is, speaking openly, and they say nothing to him! Can it be that the authorities really know that this is the Christ? ²⁷But we know where this man comes from, and when the Christ appears, no one will know where he comes from." ²⁸So Jesus proclaimed, as he taught in the temple, "You know me, and you know where I come from? But I have not come of my own accord. He who sent me is true, and him you do not know. ²⁹I know him, for I come from him, and he sent me." ³⁰So they were seeking to arrest him, but no one laid a hand on him, because his hour had not yet come. ³¹Yet many of the people believed in him. They said, "When the Christ appears, will he do more signs than this man has done?"

Officers Sent to Arrest Jesus

³²The Pharisees heard the crowd muttering these things about him, and the chief priests and Pharisees sent officers to arrest him. ³³Jesus then said, "I will be with you a little longer, and then I am going to him who sent me. ³⁴You will seek me and you will not find me. Where I am you cannot come." ³⁵The Jews said to one another, "Where does this man intend to go that we

will not find him? Does he intend to go to the Dispersion among the Greeks and teach the Greeks? [36]What does he mean by saying, 'You will seek me and you will not find me,' and, 'Where I am you cannot come'?"

Key Verse

Yet many of the people believed in him. They said, "When the Christ appears, will he do more signs than this man has done?" (John 7:31).

Rivers of Living Water

[37]On the last day of the feast, the great day, Jesus stood up and cried out, "If anyone thirsts, let him come to me and drink. [38]Whoever believes in me, as the Scripture has said, 'Out of his heart will flow rivers of living water.'" [39]Now this he said about the Spirit, whom those who believed in him were to receive, for as yet the Spirit had not been given, because Jesus was not yet glorified.

Division Among the People

[40]When they heard these words, some of the people said, "This really is the Prophet." [41]Others said, "This is the Christ." But some said, "Is the Christ to come from Galilee? [42]Has not the Scripture said that the Christ comes from the offspring of David, and comes from Bethlehem, the village where David was?" [43]So there was a division among the people over him. [44]Some of them wanted to arrest him, but no one laid hands on him.

[45]The officers then came to the chief priests and Pharisees, who said to them, "Why did you not bring him?" [46]The officers answered, "No one ever spoke like this man!" [47]The Pharisees answered them, "Have you also been deceived? [48]Have any of the authorities or the Pharisees believed in him? [49]But this crowd that does not know the law is accursed." [50]Nicodemus, who had gone to him before, and who was one of them, said to them, [51]"Does our law judge a man without first giving him a hearing and learning what he does?" [52]They replied, "Are you from Galilee too? Search and see that no prophet arises from Galilee."

Go Deeper

This chapter includes a second occasion in which Jesus talked about Himself as the source of living water. He made the same claim in John 4:10. When He was speaking during the Feast of Booths (Tabernacles or Sukkot) in Jerusalem, He added the important note that His claim was based on Scripture: "Whoever believes in me, as the Scripture has said, 'Out of his heart will flow rivers of living water'" (John 7:38). To what scriptures was Jesus referring?

If your Bible includes cross-references next to verses, you will probably find listed all or some of the following passages: Isaiah 12:3; 44:3; 58:11; Ezekiel

(continued)

Go Deeper Continued ...

47:1–10; Joel 3:18. Jesus wasn't quoting these verses but referring to their combined message that God is the source of everlasting water—life.

Part of the celebration of the Feast of Booths involved remembering how God had provided water to His people in the wilderness. All these verses make it clear that Jesus was making two claims in one with this statement. He was announcing who He was, and He was proclaiming the eternal nature of His gift. Here John explains that the gift to which Jesus was referring was His Spirit. (See John 7:39.) In what sense would you say that living water flows from your life?

I t motivates, controls and sometimes immobilizes us—the fear of rejection. How often do we make wrong decisions or hesitate to make the right decision because we dread negative reactions?

We avoid being avoided. We fear the wagging finger, the head shaking and the scathing words of disappointment. Like the sudden wailing siren and flashing lights of a police car in the rearview mirror, the possibility of rejection puts our entire body on high alert. We may even wonder sometimes what's worse: rejection itself or the fear it instills in us.

Jesus understood rejection. For Him it was never just a possibility but a certainty. Rejection was prophetically guaranteed! (See Ps. 22:7–8, 14–17; 118:22; Isa. 53.) One of John's opening remarks about Jesus was, "He came to his own, and his own people did not receive him" (John 1:11).

Even His own brothers did not accept Him. As we read this chapter, we can almost hear the mockery in their voices as they dare Jesus to show up in Jerusalem (7:3–4). They almost seem to say, "It's easy to impress the country folk around here. People in the big city are another matter!" They assumed Jesus had a flawed strategy for success. "For no one works in secret if he seeks to be known openly. If you do these things, show yourself to the world" (v. 4).

As He demonstrated repeatedly during His ministry, Jesus didn't act based on others' dares or demands, expectations or timing. His decisions were not determined by the fear of rejection or its certainty. Instead, He paid attention to His Father's directions and timetable.

So, Jesus told His brothers the same thing He told His mother when she asked Him to do something about the crisis at the wedding reception: "My time has not yet come" (v. 6). On both these occasions it's almost as if Jesus got the go-ahead from His Father almost as soon as He said no to the demands of others.

When Jesus arrived in Jerusalem, He was already the subject of intense discussions behind the scenes. John identified several groups: "the Jews" were the Jewish leaders, chief priests and Pharisees; "the people" were the crowds thronging to Jerusalem, curious and confused; and "the disciples" were a large group, including the Twelve, who were more or less following Jesus.

Within each group, arguments over Jesus' identity created chaos. Some believed, a few wondered and many were determined to disbelieve. A warrant was issued for Jesus' arrest; men were sent to take Him into custody. When they returned empty-handed and were questioned, their response captured the real heart of the situation: "No one ever spoke like this man" (v. 46).

That was Jesus' "problem." He didn't speak like other teachers. He didn't tell people what they expected to hear. That's still Jesus' "problem" today. He made more than enough wise statements to earn people's admiration, but He also made some pretty wild statements that can't be overlooked. People who call Jesus a "great teacher" have to deliberately ignore much of what He said (or claim He never said those things). He was more than a great teacher, or He was much less than a great teacher.

At least four times in this chapter Jesus made statements or asked questions that caused His listeners (and us) to make a choice about His identity:

"If anyone's will is to do God's will, he will know whether the teaching is from God or whether I am speaking on my own authority" (v. 17).

> ❝ *Jesus understood rejection. For Him it was never just a possibility but a certainty.* ❞

"Are you angry with me because on the Sabbath I made a man's whole body well?" (v. 23).

"You know me, and you know where I come from?" (v. 28).

"Whoever believes in me, as the Scripture has said, 'Out of his heart will flow rivers of living water'" (v. 38).

Jesus provoked faith or rejection. He acknowledged those who trusted and those who turned away. But He wouldn't settle for casual commitment. Even Nicodemus, whom we met back in chapter 3, made a brief appearance here (vv. 50–52), attempting to encourage a fair hearing for Jesus. Instead of answering his legitimate question, his fellow Pharisees responded with slurs against Galileans.

Before we chide Nicodemus for his lack of boldness, we need to consider how committed we are to Jesus and how openly we make that known to others in our lives. When we are at family gatherings or in workplace discussions, when the subject of religion comes up, how well do we let others know what we believe about Jesus? Perhaps Nicodemus was on his way to overcoming the fear of rejection. If so, he can be an example to us!

Express It

As you pray today, express your gratitude to Jesus for the evidences of living water in your life. Ask Him to show you ways you may be impeding the flow, and accept His help in removing those obstructions.

Consider It

As you read John 7:1–52, consider these questions:

1) What reasons do people in this chapter give for not believing in Jesus?

_____

_____

_____

2) How did His hearers first respond to Jesus as He taught in the temple (vv. 14–16)?

_____

_____

_____

3) What historical argument did Jesus raise to justify His performing a miracle of healing on the Sabbath (vv. 21–24)?

_____

_____

_____

4) What principles for wise living can we find in Jesus' statement, "Do not judge by appearances, but judge with right judgment" (v. 24)?

_____

_____

_____

5) How does Jesus' promise of living water (vv. 37–39) compare with His statements about living water to the woman at the well in chapter 4?

_____

_____

_____

6) In what way were the people described in verses 40–44 making the mistake of judging by appearances rather than right judgment (v. 24)?

_____

_____

_____

7) How does Nicodemus' question (vv. 50–51) contradict the assertion by the Pharisees (vv. 46–49)?

_____

_____

_____

Lesson **8**

Busy Rocks

Jesus lit up the world. Where He walked and talked, people saw things in a new way. They saw the truth. And they often turned away from truth. Sometimes, they turned away violently, desperate to hide from the light. Through this lesson, we'll discover how turning toward the truth will truly set us free.

John 7:53–8:59

[The earliest manuscripts do not include John 7:53–8:11]

The Woman Caught in Adultery

⁵³[[They went each to his own house, **8** but Jesus went to the Mount of Olives. ²Early in the morning he came again to the temple. All the people came to him, and he sat down and taught them. ³The scribes and the Pharisees brought a woman who had been caught in adultery, and placing her in the midst ⁴they said to him, "Teacher, this woman has been caught in the act of adultery. ⁵Now in the Law Moses commanded us to stone such women. So what do you say?" ⁶This they said to test him, that they might have some charge to bring against him. Jesus bent down and wrote with his finger on the ground. ⁷And as they continued to ask him, he stood up and said to them, "Let him who is without sin among you be the first to throw a stone at her." ⁸And once more he bent down and wrote on the ground. ⁹But when they heard it, they went away one by one, beginning with the older ones, and Jesus was left alone with the woman standing before him. ¹⁰Jesus stood up and said to her, "Woman, where are they? Has no one condemned you?" ¹¹She said, "No one, Lord." And Jesus said, "Neither do I condemn you; go, and from now on sin no more."]]

I Am the Light of the World

¹²Again Jesus spoke to them, saying, "I am the light of the world. Whoever follows me will not walk in darkness, but will have the light of life." ¹³So the Pharisees said to him, "You are bearing witness about yourself; your testimony is not true." ¹⁴Jesus answered, "Even if I do bear witness about myself, my testimony is true, for I know where I came from and where I am going, but you do not know where I come from or where I am going. ¹⁵You judge according to the flesh; I judge no one. ¹⁶Yet even if I do judge, my judgment is true, for it is not I alone who judge, but I and the Father who sent me. ¹⁷In your Law it is written that the testimony of two men is true. ¹⁸I am the one who bears witness about myself, and the Father who sent me bears witness about me." ¹⁹They said to him therefore, "Where is your Father?" Jesus answered, "You know neither me nor my Father. If you knew me, you would know my Father also." ²⁰These words he spoke in the treasury, as he taught in the temple; but no one arrested him, because his hour had not yet come.

²¹So he said to them again, "I am going away, and you will seek me, and you will die in your sin. Where I am going, you cannot come." ²²So the Jews said, "Will he kill himself, since he says, 'Where I am going, you cannot come'?" ²³He said to them, "You are from below; I am from above. You are of this world; I am not of this world. ²⁴I told you that you would die in your sins, for unless you believe that I am he you will die in your sins." ²⁵So they said to him, "Who are you?" Jesus said to them, "Just what I have been telling you from the beginning. ²⁶I have much to say about you and much to judge, but he who sent me is true, and I declare to the world what I have heard from him." ²⁷They did not understand that he had been speaking to them about the Father. ²⁸So Jesus said to them, "When you have lifted up the Son of Man, then you will know that I am he, and that I do nothing on my own authority, but speak just as the Father taught me. ²⁹And he who sent me is with me. He has not left me alone, for I always do the things that are pleasing to him." ³⁰As he was saying these things, many believed in him.

The Truth Will Set You Free

³¹So Jesus said to the Jews who had believed in him, "If you abide in my word, you are truly my disciples, ³²and you will know the truth, and the truth will set you

free." [33]They answered him, "We are off-spring of Abraham and have never been enslaved to anyone. How is it that you say, 'You will become free'?"

[34]Jesus answered them, "Truly, truly, I say to you, everyone who commits sin is a slave to sin. [35]The slave does not remain in the house forever; the son remains forever. [36]So if the Son sets you free, you will be free indeed. [37]I know that you are off-spring of Abraham; yet you seek to kill me because my word finds no place in you. [38]I speak of what I have seen with my Father, and you do what you have heard from your father."

> # Key Verse
>
> If you abide in my word, you are truly my disciples, and you will know the truth, and the truth will set you free" (John 8:31–32).

You Are of Your Father the Devil

[39]They answered him, "Abraham is our father." Jesus said to them, "If you were Abraham's children, you would be doing what Abraham did, [40]but now you seek to kill me, a man who has told you the truth that I heard from God. This is not what Abraham did. [41]You are doing what your father did." They said to him, "We were not born of sexual immorality. We have one Father—even God." [42]Jesus said to them, "If God were your Father, you would love me, for I came from God and I am here. I came not of my own accord, but he sent me. [43]Why do you not understand what I say? It is because you cannot bear to hear my word. [44]You are of your father the devil, and your will is to do your father's desires. He was a murderer from the beginning, and has nothing to do with the truth, because there is no truth in him. When he lies, he speaks out of his own character, for he is a liar and the father of lies. [45]But because I tell the truth, you do not believe me. [46]Which one of you convicts me of sin? If I tell the truth, why do you not believe me? [47]Whoever is of God hears the words of God. The reason why you do not hear them is that you are not of God."

Before Abraham Was, I Am

[48]The Jews answered him, "Are we not right in saying that you are a Samaritan and have a demon?" [49]Jesus answered, "I do not have a demon, but I honor my Father, and you dishonor me. [50]Yet I do not seek my own glory; there is One who seeks it, and he is the judge. [51]Truly, truly, I say to you, if anyone keeps my word, he will never see death." [52]The Jews said to him, "Now we know that you have a demon! Abraham died, as did the prophets, yet you say, 'If anyone keeps my word, he will never taste death.' [53]Are you greater than our father Abraham, who died? And the prophets died! Who do you make yourself out to be?" [54]Jesus answered, "If I glorify myself, my glory is nothing. It is my Father who glorifies me, of whom you say, 'He is our God.' [55]But you have not known him. I know him. If I were to say that I do not know him, I would be a liar like you, but I do know him and I keep his word. [56]Your father Abraham rejoiced that he would see my day. He saw it and was glad." [57]So the Jews said to him, "You are not yet fifty years old, and have you seen Abraham?" [58]Jesus said to them, "Truly, truly, I say to you, before Abraham was, I am." [59]So they picked up stones to throw at him, but Jesus hid himself and went out of the temple.

Go Deeper

What does it mean to "abide"? John recorded the many times Jesus used the term (6:56, 8:31, 15:4–10). The word translates a Greek word that can also mean, "to stay, remain or continue." The verb is used with two directions, indicating an action that occurs in or to us—"Whoever feeds on my flesh and drinks my blood abides in me, and I in him" (6:56)—and an action that we do—"If you keep my commandments, you will abide in my love" (15:10).

Jesus makes "abide in my word" (getting to know Him intimately through God's Word) a test for true disciples (8:31). It sets up the famous words, "and you will know the truth, and the truth will set you free" (v. 32). His audience began to argue about the issue of freedom, but Jesus answered with an explanation of "abiding": "The slave does not remain in the house forever; the son remains forever. So if the Son sets you free, you will be free indeed" (vv. 35–36).

The word "remain" is the same word translated "abide" above. Abiding/remaining in Jesus' word is like abiding in His house, where He lives. The closer we are to living out and obeying Jesus' words, the more we will experience His presence.

The eighth chapter of the Gospel of John begins and ends with stones. The scene opens with an early morning stoning-in-the-making featuring a woman caught in adultery. By the end of the discussion, the crowd forgot the woman because now they wanted to stone Jesus.

We know from the last couple of chapters that a lot was going on behind-the-scenes. The Pharisees and Sadducees were holding strategy sessions to try to catch Jesus in a mistake. Jesus had such a reputation for compassion that someone finally suggested they give Him an impossible problem to solve. With the right circumstances, they might get Jesus to betray Himself.

Their plan was brilliant. Confront Jesus with an obviously guilty party, and make Him choose between compassion and the Law. Either choice would land Him in hot water. If He let the guilty one escape punishment, they would have a case for lawbreaking against Jesus. If He passed judgment, they could blame Him for starting a ruckus that would provoke the Roman officials. They thought they finally had a solution for their "Jesus problem."

Apparently, they identified a woman with a reputation and arranged for a man to have a rendezvous with her. Only the woman (not the man, as the Law also required) would be a pawn in the plan. They managed impeccable timing, for they not only caught the woman "in the act" but also immediately dragged her to Jesus.

Everything went just as planned until they confronted Jesus and waited for His answer. He caught them completely by surprise. His response let them know that they were just as liable for His judgment as the woman. He *knew* they were just as implicated (perhaps even more so) as the woman—they were accomplices in her sin and guilty of betraying her. In order to rightfully stone the woman, they would also have to stone themselves! Meanwhile, we can only guess what He was jotting in the sand. The combination of His challenge and their consciences got the better of them, and they dropped their stones and walked away.

Before He let her go, Jesus made it clear to the woman that while He hadn't condemned her, He didn't condone her sin either. Moments away from a terrible death, this woman got an opportunity to "go, and from now on sin no more" (John 8:11). Did she walk away that day intending to discover how this man could help her deal with sin in a new way?

Most of us avoid identifying with either the woman or her accusers in this passage. The first involves too much pain. The second, too much shame. In practice, we often take the role of accuser as a way to avoid being accused. We are quick to find fault and slow to forgive. We assume that by focusing on people whose sins are greater than ours, we'll somehow feel better about ourselves. Meanwhile, our own sins eat away at our souls.

Jesus confronted His challengers with their own spiritual needs. When we're declaring someone guilty and beyond forgiveness, the last thing we want to think about is our own sinfulness! But we dare not forget that we never outgrow our need for a Savior.

The rest of this chapter reminds us why Jesus can treat us the same way He treated that sinful woman. He is light and speaks truth. In His presence, we will see and hear the truth (even if we don't want to listen). To our amazement, when we turn toward Jesus as light and truth, we find, not condemnation, but grace and forgiveness. These verses include two of the great "I am" statements Jesus made: "I am the light of the world" (8:12) and "Truly, truly, I say to you, before Abraham was, I am" (v. 58).

This brings us to this lesson's key verse. Jesus described a progression by which we gain true freedom: 1) "abide in my word," 2) live as "my disciples," 3) "know the truth" and 4) "the truth will set you free." In this context, the words we need to "abide in" are "I am the light of the world" and "before Abraham was, I am."

How do we "abide"? We take Jesus' words to heart. We trust them and Him implicitly. We don't demand to understand or know everything before we trust. We listen to Jesus and trust. The more we do that, the more we experience light flooding our lives. The more we experience light, the more we live by truth. And the more we live by truth, the more we know that when truth uncovers sin in our lives, Jesus is waiting to forgive, cleanse and send us on our way with His presence as we "go and sin no more." Indeed, the truth does set us free.

Express It

As you prepare to pray, review some of the times in your life when Jesus has demonstrated Himself to be your light and your source of truth. Those may have been difficult times, but God proved Himself faithful to you. Consider whether there are places in your life where His light and truth are shining, but you haven't yet given proper attention. Talk to Him about what you need to do to more consistently abide in His word.

Consider It

As you read John 7:53–8:59, consider these questions:

1) What might have been some of the woman's observations about her encounter with Jesus?

_____

_____

_____

_____

2) In what ways has Jesus helped you deal with sin in your life?

_____

_____

_____

_____

3) Describe the argument that followed Jesus' statement about being the light of the world. What points did Jesus make?

_____

_____

_____

_____

4) Why does Jesus question the right of the crowd to claim Abraham as their father?

_____

_____

_____

_____

5) In this chapter, how did Jesus describe His role in setting people free?

_____

_____

_____

_____

6) What is it about Jesus saying, "before Abraham was, I am" (8:58) that would cause the crowd to pick up stones to kill Him?

_____

_____

_____

_____

Lesson
9

What Do You Know?

John 9 is like a summary for a TV mini-series. It includes all the parts for a gripping story. A man's sad life is interrupted by a miracle no one seems to be able to accept except the man! Both the man and his questioners want to find out who did the miracle, but for very different reasons. The story ends with sight for one man and "blindness" for the others.

John 9:1–41

Jesus Heals a Man Born Blind

9 As he passed by, he saw a man blind from birth. [2]And his disciples asked him, "Rabbi, who sinned, this man or his parents, that he was born blind?" [3]Jesus answered, "It was not that this man sinned, or his parents, but that the works of God might be displayed in him. [4]We must work the works of him who sent me while it is day; night is coming, when no one can work. [5]As long as I am in the world, I am the light of the world." [6]Having said these things, he spat on the ground and made mud with the saliva. Then he anointed the man's eyes with the mud [7]and said to him, "Go, wash in the pool of Siloam" (which means Sent). So he went and washed and came back seeing.

[8]The neighbors and those who had seen him before as a beggar were saying, "Is this not the man who used to sit and beg?" [9]Some said, "It is he." Others said, "No, but he is like him." He kept saying, "I am the man." [10]So they said to him, "Then how were your eyes opened?" [11]He answered, "The man called Jesus made mud and anointed my eyes and said to me, 'Go to Siloam and wash.' So I went and washed and received my sight." [12]They said to him, "Where is he?" He said, "I do not know."

[13]They brought to the Pharisees the man who had formerly been blind. [14]Now it was a Sabbath day when Jesus made the mud and opened his eyes. [15]So the Pharisees again asked him how he had received his sight. And he said to them, "He put mud on my eyes, and I washed, and I see." [16]Some of the Pharisees said, "This man is not from God, for he does not keep the Sabbath." But others said, "How can a man who is a sinner do such signs?" And there was a division among them. [17]So they said again to the blind man, "What do you say about him, since he has opened your eyes?" He said, "He is a prophet."

[18]The Jews did not believe that he had been blind and had received his sight, until they called the parents of the man who had received his sight [19]and asked them, "Is this your son, who you say was born blind? How then does he now see?" [20]His parents answered, "We know that this is our son and that he was born blind. [21]But how he now sees we do not know, nor do we know who opened his eyes. Ask him; he is of age. He will speak for himself." [22](His parents said these things because they feared the Jews, for the Jews had already agreed that if anyone should confess Jesus to be Christ, he was to be put out of

> ## Key Verse
>
> *He answered, "Whether he is a sinner I do not know. One thing I do know, that though I was blind, now I see" (John 9:25).*

the synagogue.) [23]Therefore his parents said, "He is of age; ask him."

[24]So for the second time they called the man who had been blind and said to him, "Give glory to God. We know that this man is a sinner." [25]He answered, "Whether he is a sinner I do not know. One thing I do know, that though I was blind, now I see." [26]They said to him, "What did he do to you? How did he open your eyes?" [27]He an-

swered them, "I have told you already, and you would not listen. Why do you want to hear it again? Do you also want to become his disciples?" 28And they reviled him, saying, "You are his disciple, but we are disciples of Moses. 29We know that God has spoken to Moses, but as for this man, we do not know where he comes from." 30The man answered, "Why, this is an amazing thing! You do not know where he comes from, and yet he opened my eyes. 31We know that God does not listen to sinners, but if anyone is a worshiper of God and does his will, God listens to him. 32Never since the world began has it been heard that anyone opened the eyes of a man born blind. 33If this man were not from God, he could do nothing." 34They answered him, "You were born in utter sin, and would you teach us?" And they cast him out.

35Jesus heard that they had cast him out, and having found him he said, "Do you believe in the Son of Man?" 36He answered, "And who is he, sir, that I may believe in him?" 37Jesus said to him, "You have seen him, and it is he who is speaking to you." 38He said, "Lord, I believe," and he worshiped him. 39Jesus said, "For judgment I came into this world, that those who do not see may see, and those who see may become blind." 40Some of the Pharisees near him heard these things, and said to him, "Are we also blind?" 41Jesus said to them, "If you were blind, you would have no guilt; but now that you say, 'We see,' your guilt remains."

Go Deeper

This chapter begins and ends with blind men. The man we met in the first verses received his sight from Jesus. The men we met throughout the chapter refused to really look at Jesus, and so they became increasingly blind. And they didn't appreciate Jesus' pointing out this fact to them. This "both ways" process was described by Jesus in 9:39: "For judgment I came into this world, that those who do not see may see, and those who see may become blind." This explains in part what Jesus meant earlier in the chapter when He said, "As long as I am in the world, I am the light of the world" (9:5).

This is the second time Jesus describes Himself as "the light of the world" (8:12). Consider some of the other connections between Jesus and light in the Gospel of John (1:4–5, 7–9; 3:19–21; 5:35; 8:12; 11:9–10; 12:35–36,46). What do you mean when you tell Jesus, "You are my light"?

Close your eyes for a moment and imagine what it would sound like to hear someone spit very near you. What would you think if you suddenly felt a wet paste that smelled like fresh mud wiped over your eyelids?

The man we meet in John 9 couldn't see. As far as we know, all his other senses and his brain were in excellent working order. He probably heard very clearly the disciples asking Jesus a loaded question: "Rabbi, who sinned, this man or his parents, that he was born blind?" (John 9:2).

In their minds, there were only two possibilities. One possibility was that the man's parents had done a bad thing, so the baby was born sightless. There were even Jewish scholars in Jesus' day who believed that a baby could commit a sin in the womb. So, maybe the man himself was at fault. The disciples wanted Jesus to settle the issue. He did, but as usual, He did it in a way they didn't expect.

In modern language, Jesus gave them an answer outside the box. It wasn't someone's fault; the man's blindness was part of God's plan, "that the works of God might be displayed in him" (9:3). This chapter is a New Testament condensed version of the grand drama of the Book of Job. Terrible things happened to a man. Then his friends showed up to comfort him and help him figure out how he had offended God. Job couldn't honestly think of a way he had offended God. But his friends insisted someone was at fault, and Job was the only one left to blame! Then God spoke up and settled the issue.

Some things are beyond figuring out. It doesn't mean that wrong actions don't yield bad results, or sowing bad seed doesn't yield a harvest of bad crops. But not all disappointing harvests come from bad seeds. Other factors (most of them under God's control) determine the quality of the harvest.

Jesus told neither the disciples nor the man what He was about to do. He used His own spit to make mud from Jerusalem dirt and smeared it on the man's eyes. Then He sent the man off to the Pool of Siloam to wash. Note that the items Jesus used in His miracles were never random or impulsive. His choice here reminds us that we are basically dust. When Jesus used mud as a salve, He was actually applying the original Manufacturer's replacement parts. (See Gen. 2:7.)

Jesus was true to His word. He *is* light, and He brought the light of sight into the man's life. The man, now seeing, returned home to face a gauntlet of unbelief! His neighbors said he looked familiar, but it couldn't be him. (Apparently they couldn't believe *their* eyes!) He described what happened, and they insisted he go to the Pharisees to make the healing legitimate. Obviously, he knew Jesus' name but hadn't seen Him yet.

With the Pharisees, everything was about the Sabbath. For many of them, keeping the Sabbath was more important than healing a man who had been blind all his life. But some couldn't help but wonder who Jesus was that He could exercise such miraculous compassion.

Notice how the intense questioning of the Pharisees forced the man to sharpen his understanding of Jesus. The first time he was asked to identify his healer, he said, "The man called Jesus" (John 9:11). The next time he was confronted, he said, "He is a prophet" (9:17). His healing was called into question. His parents were put on the spot. For a third time, he was cross-examined about Jesus. By this point he was thoroughly disgusted with the treatment he received. He told them with unshakable conviction, "One thing I do know, that though I was blind, now I see" (v. 25).

When it came to common-sense conclusions about Jesus based on His actions, the highly educated theologians just couldn't keep up with the man who had been healed. After all, they were dealing solely in the realm of theory while the blind

> *" If you have 'experienced' receiving light in your life from Jesus, never back down from those who deny the light because they have not experienced it. "*

man was responding from his experience. If you have "experienced" receiving light in your life from Jesus, never back down from those who deny that light because they have not experienced it. Remember, the person with an experience is never at the mercy of the person with an argument.

At this point, Jesus sought him out. He needed to take one more step in his understanding. The Lord approached the man with a question. The voice he remembered now came with a face he would never forget. "Do you believe in the Son of Man?" Jesus asked (v. 35). When the man expressed a desire to believe, Jesus introduced Himself. The man's inner eyes were opened, and he said, "Lord, I believe" (v. 38). His journey toward meeting Jesus is exactly the same one each of us takes or misses, to our great gain or loss.

Express It

When you close your eyes to pray, you are accepting temporary physical blindness in order to more fully concentrate on being aware of Jesus. How do you use your other senses in prayer? Do they become sharper? Have you ever thanked Jesus for what you smelled during prayer? How often do you deliberately try to listen for Jesus' voice, both with your ears and with your soul? Do that today.

Consider It

As you read John 9:1–41, consider these questions:

1) Why is punishment the first cause we consider when something bad happens?

_____

_____

_____

_____

2) Even if healing doesn't take place, how can a disability bring glory to God?

_____

_____

_____

_____

3) What are some of the parallels between physical and spiritual blindness?

_____

_____

_____

_____

4) Why was this former blind man so convinced Jesus was from God?

_____

_____

_____

_____

5) How do you respond when someone questions your experience with Christ?

_____

_____

_____

_____

6) In what ways do you identify with the man's gradual growth in understanding Jesus?

_____

_____

_____

_____

Meeting the Good Shepherd

Toddlers choose a wide variety of expressions as their first intelligible words. "Mama" or "Dada" is always a crowd pleaser, but kids have a way of picking a first word that can baffle and delight parents and assorted other observers. Older children are much more unanimous in their choice of first phrases: "I'll do it myself!" is a common one. As we see in this lesson, the innate independence we bring into the world meets its match in the Good Shepherd.

John 10:1–42

I Am the Good Shepherd

10 "Truly, truly, I say to you, he who does not enter the sheepfold by the door but climbs in by another way, that man is a thief and a robber. [2]But he who enters by the door is the shepherd of the sheep. [3]To him the gatekeeper opens. The sheep hear his voice, and he calls his own sheep by name and leads them out. [4]When he has brought out all his own, he goes before them, and the sheep follow him, for they know his voice. [5]A stranger they will not follow, but they will flee from him, for they do not know the voice of strangers." [6]This figure of speech Jesus used with them, but they did not understand what he was saying to them.

[7]So Jesus again said to them, "Truly, truly, I say to you, I am the door of the sheep. [8]All who came before me are thieves and robbers, but the sheep did not listen to them. [9]I am the door. If anyone enters by me, he will be saved and will go in and out and find pasture. [10]The thief comes only to steal and kill and destroy. I came that they may have life and have it abundantly. [11]I am the good shepherd. The good shepherd lays down his life for the sheep. [12]He who is a hired hand and not a shepherd, who does not own the sheep, sees the wolf coming and leaves the sheep and flees, and the wolf snatches them and scatters them. [13]He flees because he is a hired hand and cares nothing for the sheep. [14]I am the good shepherd. I know my own and my own know me, [15]just as the Father knows me and I know the Father; and I lay down my life for the sheep. [16]And I have other sheep that are not of this fold. I must bring them also, and they will listen to my voice. So there will be one flock, one shepherd. [17]For this reason the Father loves me, because I lay down my life that I may take it up again. [18]No one takes it from me, but I lay it down of my own accord. I have authority to lay it down, and I have authority to take it up again. This charge I have received from my Father."

[19]There was again a division among the Jews because of these words. [20]Many of them said, "He has a demon, and is insane; why listen to him?" [21]Others said, "These are not the words of one who is oppressed by a demon. Can a demon open the eyes of the blind?"

Key Verse

"I am the good shepherd. The good shepherd lays down his life for the sheep" (John 10:11).

I and the Father Are One

[22]At that time the Feast of Dedication took place at Jerusalem. It was winter, [23]and Jesus was walking in the temple, in the colonnade of Solomon. [24]So the Jews gathered around him and said to him, "How long will you keep us in suspense? If you are the Christ, tell us plainly." [25]Jesus answered them, "I told you, and you do not believe. The works that I do in my Father's name bear witness about me, [26]but you do not believe because you are not part of my flock. [27]My sheep hear my voice, and I know them, and they follow me. [28]I give them eternal life, and they will never perish, and no one will snatch them out of my hand. [29]My Father, who has given them

to me, is greater than all, and no one is able to snatch them out of the Father's hand. [30]I and the Father are one."

[31]The Jews picked up stones again to stone him. [32]Jesus answered them, "I have shown you many good works from the Father; for which of them are you going to stone me?" [33]The Jews answered him, "It is not for a good work that we are going to stone you but for blasphemy, because you, being a man, make yourself God." [34]Jesus answered them, "Is it not written in your Law, 'I said, you are gods'? [35]If he called them gods to whom the word of God came—and Scripture cannot be broken— [36]do you say of him whom the Father consecrated and sent into the world, 'You are blaspheming,' because I said, 'I am the Son of God'? [37]If I am not doing the works of my Father, then do not believe me; [38]but if I do them, even though you do not believe me, believe the works, that you may know and understand that the Father is in me and I am in the Father." [39]Again they sought to arrest him, but he escaped from their hands.

[40]He went away again across the Jordan to the place where John had been baptizing at first, and there he remained. [41]And many came to him. And they said, "John did no sign, but everything that John said about this man was true." [42]And many believed in him there.

Go Deeper

Jesus began John 10 with a warning about thieves and robbers. Before introducing Himself as the Good Shepherd, He cautioned His audience about other shepherds. The Bible is filled with images of illegitimate shepherds, shepherds who abandon the sheep and shepherds who abuse their sheep. The Jews knew all about these images.

Jeremiah 23:1 says, "'Woe to the shepherds who destroy and scatter the sheep of my pasture!' declares the LORD." Isaiah cried, "They are shepherds who have no understanding; they have all turned to their own way, each to his own gain, one and all" (Isa. 56:11). So, the whole concept of a greedy, illegitimate shepherd was well known to these Jewish people.

Jesus was referring to the entry of the robber, the false teacher and the false religious leader (John 10:7–15). That person who sneaks over the wall of the sheepfold is not a legitimate shepherd. Jesus is warning us about those who claim revelation from God but have no way to prove that revelation. Their lives do not give any evidence of truth. They just ask you to believe. Such shepherds never come close to passing the test of the Good Shepherd who laid down His life for the sheep.

The comparison is painfully true and not at all flattering: We are like sheep. Jesus said, "I am the Good Shepherd," but he never quite said, "you are the sheep." The identity of "sheep-hood" is a privilege we get to adopt for ourselves. It describes how we act in life and how we must respond to Jesus. We can't recognize Jesus as the Good Shepherd unless we get to the place where we begin to understand that we are sheep.

That's exactly what David did when he wrote the famous 23rd Psalm. It's so familiar that we seldom think about the words. "The Lord is my shepherd" (v. 1) includes two powerful and necessary titles about God's role in our lives. We tend to skip over the first and leap to the second.

"Shepherd" does have a comforting, protective sound. But the truth is, if we fail to recognize God as Lord, as the One actually in charge, we will have a difficult time experiencing Him as Shepherd. Instead, He will seem like a stranger.

Lots of people want to make the "Shepherd" part primary and the "Lord" part optional. But wanting to have a Shepherd who isn't Lord only shows that we don't understand the meaning of Shepherd or Lord! Jesus' teaching in John 10 helps us realize that we definitely need the Lord who is the Good Shepherd.

How do we recognize we are sheep? Well, we certainly tend to get lost if we strike out on our own. Going our way usually starts out feeling right, but ends up being wrong. We are prone to follow even the wrong leader if he seems to know where he is going. A leader's voice may sound like good direction until we discover we are as lost as he is. Jesus speaks a new voice into our lives—the voice we were created to hear and obey.

Years ago I had the opportunity to see this passage illustrated in the Holy Land while we were filming a video for Back to the Bible. For one particular shot, we set up in a Bedouin shepherd's cave sheepfold. The shepherd and a dozen sheep were on hand for videotaping.

I took a position in the cave, and when the film crew said, "Action!" I did my best impression of a shepherd. I called, coaxed and tried to bribe the sheep to come into the cave (their home). I used my friendliest and most persuasive voice. The sheep didn't budge. I did everything I could think of to woo the sheep, but they never moved. Then the Bedouin and I switched places. He made a couple of soft noises with his mouth, and the sheep immediately abandoned me and joined him. They knew their master's voice and wanted his company.

The Good Shepherd, according to John 10:4, is the genuine shepherd who leads His sheep. And the sheep follow Him because they know His voice. Jesus' original hearers were very familiar with shepherds and sheep. But verse 6 tells us they didn't get Jesus' point. Why? Because they, like us, were probably reluctant to identify with sheep!

So, Jesus switched analogies: same setting, different role. "I am the door of the sheep," Jesus said (10:7). Then He repeated the phrase but left out "sheep." "I am the door. If anyone enters by me, he will be saved and will go in and out and find pasture" (v. 9). Jesus provides the voice we follow and the way to go. We may not know exactly what Jesus meant by "sheep," but it takes a lot of effort to exclude ourselves from the term "anyone."

And yet Jesus is presenting a choice. Those who enter by Jesus will: 1) be saved, 2) go in and out and 3) find pasture (see v. 9). Jesus promises eternal results (salvation) and present benefits (going in and out in life with God's provision) to those who let Him be their door. But those who do *not* enter by Jesus will not experience the same results. Later Jesus highlighted the importance of the choice when He said, "I am the way, and the truth, and the life. No one comes to the Father except through me" (14:6).

Once He showed us the door, He resumed His role as the Shepherd (see 10:11) who lays down His life for the sheep. In the verses that follow, Jesus made it clear that He willingly placed His life on the line "for the sheep"—for us. Most people who surrounded Jesus, even His disciples, failed to grasp what He was saying. It only made life-changing sense after the Resurrection. That's when the sheep finally got it! And the sheep today are still

> **"Lots of people want to make the 'Shepherd' part primary and the 'Lord' part optional. But wanting to have a Shepherd who isn't Lord only shows that we don't understand the meaning of Shepherd or Lord!"**

"getting it"!

The question is, have you gotten it? Or are you still insisting about life, "I can do it myself!"

Express It

As you pray, think about the ways you picture Jesus in your mind. Practice talking to Jesus in one of His specific roles. Consider using His role as the Good Shepherd. One way to start is to use Psalm 23, expressing the entire Psalm in the first person. (Note that verses 4–5 are already in first person.) For example: "Lord, You are my shepherd, I shall not want …"

Consider It

As you read John 10:1–42, consider these questions:

1) What else do you know about sheep that make them a good stand-in for humans?

_____

_____

_____

2) Why do the sheep refuse to follow a stranger?

_____

_____

_____

3) How did various groups respond to Jesus' words about the Good Shepherd?

_____

_____

_____

4) How does the Good Shepherd passage help you understand the "I and the Father are one" passage in the second part of this chapter?

_____

_____

_____

5) Identify the promises Jesus makes to us in this chapter.

_____

_____

_____

6) In what ways have you experienced Jesus as Lord and Shepherd?

_____

_____

_____

7) How do you hear Jesus' voice?

_____

_____

_____

Do You Believe This?

Jesus didn't show up. His friend was sick, and His other friends sent word, but Jesus didn't come. In fact, He deliberately delayed. What would you think if someone did this to you?

John 11:1–57

The Death of Lazarus

11 Now a certain man was ill, Lazarus of Bethany, the village of Mary and her sister Martha. [2]It was Mary who anointed the Lord with ointment and wiped his feet with her hair, whose brother Lazarus was ill. [3]So the sisters sent to him, saying, "Lord, he whom you love is ill." [4]But when Jesus heard it he said, "This illness does not lead to death. It is for the glory of God, so that the Son of God may be glorified through it."

[5]Now Jesus loved Martha and her sister and Lazarus. [6]So, when he heard that Lazarus was ill, he stayed two days longer in the place where he was. [7]Then after this he said to the disciples, "Let us go to Judea again." [8]The disciples said to him, "Rabbi, the Jews were just now seeking to stone you, and are you going there again?" [9]Jesus answered, "Are there not twelve hours in the day? If anyone walks in the day, he does not stumble, because he sees the light of this world. [10]But if anyone walks in the night, he stumbles, because the light is not in him." [11]After saying these things, he said to them, "Our friend Lazarus has fallen asleep, but I go to awaken him." [12]The disciples said to him, "Lord, if he has fallen asleep, he will recover." [13]Now Jesus had spoken of his death, but they thought that he meant taking rest in sleep. [14]Then Jesus told them plainly, "Lazarus has died, [15]and for your sake I am glad that I was not there, so that you may believe. But let us go to him." [16]So Thomas, called the Twin, said to his fellow disciples, "Let us also go, that we may die with him."

I Am the Resurrection and the Life

[17]Now when Jesus came, he found that Lazarus had already been in the tomb four days. [18]Bethany was near Jerusalem, about two miles off, [19]and many of the Jews had come to Martha and Mary to console them concerning their brother. [20]So when Martha heard that Jesus was coming, she went and met him, but Mary remained seated in the house. [21]Martha said to Jesus, "Lord, if you had been here, my brother would not have died. [22]But even now I know that whatever you ask from God, God will give you." [23]Jesus said to her, "Your brother will rise again." [24]Martha said to him, "I know that he will rise again in the resurrection on the last day." [25]Jesus said to her, "I am the resurrection and the life. Whoever believes in me, though he die, yet shall he live, [26]and everyone who lives and believes in me shall never die. Do you believe this?" [27]She said to him, "Yes, Lord; I believe that you are the Christ, the Son of God, who is coming into the world."

> # Key Verse
>
> *Jesus said to her, "I am the resurrection and the life. Whoever believes in me, though he die, yet shall he live, and everyone who lives and believes in me shall never die. Do you believe this?" (John 11:25–26).*

Jesus Wept

[28]When she had said this, she went and called her sister Mary, saying in private,

"The Teacher is here and is calling for you." [29]And when she heard it, she rose quickly and went to him. [30]Now Jesus had not yet come into the village, but was still in the place where Martha had met him. [31]When the Jews who were with her in the house, consoling her, saw Mary rise quickly and go out, they followed her, supposing that she was going to the tomb to weep there. [32]Now when Mary came to where Jesus was and saw him, she fell at his feet, saying to him, "Lord, if you had been here, my brother would not have died." [33]When Jesus saw her weeping, and the Jews who had come with her also weeping, he was deeply moved in his spirit and greatly troubled. [34]And he said, "Where have you laid him?" They said to him, "Lord, come and see." [35]Jesus wept. [36]So the Jews said, "See how he loved him!" [37]But some of them said, "Could not he who opened the eyes of the blind man also have kept this man from dying?"

Jesus Raises Lazarus

[38]Then Jesus, deeply moved again, came to the tomb. It was a cave, and a stone lay against it. [39]Jesus said, "Take away the stone." Martha, the sister of the dead man, said to him, "Lord, by this time there will be an odor, for he has been dead four days." [40]Jesus said to her, "Did I not tell you that if you believed you would see the glory of God?" [41]So they took away the stone. And Jesus lifted up his eyes and said, "Father, I thank you that you have heard me. [42]I knew that you always hear me, but I said this on account of the people standing around, that they may believe that you sent me." [43]When he had said these things, he cried out with a loud voice, "Lazarus, come out." [44]The man who had died came out, his hands and feet bound with linen strips, and his face wrapped with a cloth. Jesus said to them, "Unbind him, and let him go."

The Plot to Kill Jesus

[45]Many of the Jews therefore, who had come with Mary and had seen what he did, believed in him, [46]but some of them went to the Pharisees and told them what Jesus had done. [47]So the chief priests and the Pharisees gathered the Council and said, "What are we to do? For this man performs many signs. [48]If we let him go on like this, everyone will believe in him, and the Romans will come and take away both our place and our nation." [49]But one of them, Caiaphas, who was high priest that year, said to them, "You know nothing at all. [50]Nor do you understand that it is better for you that one man should die for the people, not that the whole nation should perish." [51]He did not say this of his own accord, but being high priest that year he prophesied that Jesus would die for the nation, [52]and not for the nation only, but also to gather into one the children of God who are scattered abroad. [53]So from that day on they made plans to put him to death.

[54]Jesus therefore no longer walked openly among the Jews, but went from there to the region near the wilderness, to a town called Ephraim, and there he stayed with the disciples.

[55]Now the Passover of the Jews was at hand, and many went up from the country to Jerusalem before the Passover to purify themselves. [56]They were looking for Jesus and saying to one another as they stood in the temple, "What do you think? That he will not come to the feast at all?" [57]Now the chief priests and the Pharisees had given orders that if anyone knew where he was, he should let them know, so that they might arrest him.

Go Deeper

God cried. That's not the first impression we associate with God. Since we connect tears with weakness, helplessness, pain and fear, we may hesitate to say that God can experience these things. But Philippians 2:5–11 describes the process by which God the Son emptied Himself and became one of us humans. He put on full humanity with all its weaknesses, stresses and experiences. He cried, thirsted, laughed, hungered and felt the full range of human life. He didn't exempt Himself from exposure to anything, including death.

When we pray, we are speaking to someone who knows us and our experiences inside out. That's why Hebrews 4:15–16 offers such comfort and confidence: "For we do not have a high priest who is unable to sympathize with our weaknesses, but one who in every respect has been tempted as we are, yet without sin. Let us then with confidence draw near to the throne of grace, that we may receive mercy and find grace to help in time of need."

Prayer takes on added weight in the presence of death. It's our last defense against death. When care and medicine have been exhausted, prayer remains. Those who trust in God pray all along, but all of us reach that place of crisis where praying is all we can do. We feel helpless, vulnerable and utterly dependent on God. That's not a good time to start trying to figure out what we believe about prayer. That question has to be settled long before that. Otherwise, when unsettling times come, prayer will not accomplish its purpose.

When Mary and Martha sent word to Jesus that Lazarus was dying, they had reached a prayer crisis. Jesus was their last resort. They had good reason to believe that if He arrived before death, all would be well. After all, they had heard and seen Jesus do amazing things.

John gives us a split screen view of this story. We see events move forward in Bethany as we watch Jesus in action across the Jordan River (John 10:40). Shortly after the messenger was sent to Jesus, Lazarus died. Grief consumed his sisters and those around them. In a hot region like the Middle East, bodies can't be left unburied for long. They are buried the same day.

Meanwhile, when Jesus got the message, He responded with a prediction, a promise and a postponement. He said, "This illness does not lead to death" (11:4). It didn't; it led right *through* death! He also promised that He would be glorified through the sickness. Then He postponed His departure for Judea for two more days. When the need was so obvious, why would God delay?

Jesus was never behind events, but always ahead of them. He wasn't surprised by setbacks; He never had to play catch-up. Something terrible did happen (Lazarus' death), and then something truly wonderful occurred when Jesus called His friend back from the dead.

But before the fireworks, Jesus had some faith-work in mind for the two sisters. The hard experiences in life impose a tough question: Why would God who loves us allow us to go through such difficulty? Mary and Martha must have agonized together about that question. Though they met Jesus separately as He approached their home, both sisters said exactly the same thing to Him: "Lord, if you had been here, my brother would not have died" (vv. 21,32). This was a rebuke wrapped in a compliment. "You could have done something, but You weren't here! Why not? You let us down."

The statement makes several understandable but incorrect assumptions: 1) that Jesus didn't do something; 2) that Jesus wasn't there and 3) that God's presence automatically means nothing bad can happen. But Jesus did do something—He waited. Jesus was not physically present; but He knew exactly what was happening. God drew very near even as those two sisters lovingly wrapped their brother in linen soaked in spices and tears. And we know what God did then because we know what Jesus did as He stood outside that grave—He wept. God's presence in this fallen and broken world does not mean that terrible things won't happen. We live in terrible territory, and sin makes certain that every rose we find will be accompanied by sharp thorns.

Jesus' wonderful declaration in this lesson's key verse doesn't promise that death can be avoided. He made an even better guarantee—that death won't get the last word. Those who believe in Jesus may go through death, but they will also experience resurrection! They will know exactly what the apostle Paul meant by this unforgettable phrase: "Death is swallowed up in victory" (1 Cor. 15:54).

God never withholds anything from us out of cruelty or capriciousness. He only lets us go through what seems to be the worst because He has something better in store. He won't allow us to settle for what we think will satisfy us. He knows better, even if we can't believe it at the moment. Sometimes we can hardly believe it when the better comes! And sometimes, sadly, we balk at His will and end up spending way too long in the wilderness of a hard experience that He allowed for our good.

When Jesus called Lazarus out of the grave, the effects of the sinful world did not cease. Some say Jesus wept in part because He knew Lazarus would have to go through this dying thing all over again! But death was reversed in this instance to show again that it can be defeated. It made Jesus' own Resurrection something people should have expected but didn't. The vivid pictures of linen-bound Lazarus hopping into the daylight and the glorious risen Christ bursting from His tomb still present us with a life-changing question: Do you believe this?

Express It

As you pray, ask God for a growing freedom to seek Him in all things and the faithfulness to expect Him to do not what you think best, but what He thinks best. Describe to the Lord what you want to mean when you say, "Not my will, but Yours be done." Then trust Him with the desperate needs in your life.

Consider It
As you read John 11:1–57, consider these questions:

1) **What did Jesus accomplish by waiting to visit Lazarus?**

2) **How do verses 5, 33, 35, 38 and 43 help you understand Jesus' emotional state?**

3) **Based on this chapter, how would you describe Mary's and Martha's faith?**

4) **What glimpse of the disciples' faith comes through this chapter?**

5) **Describe what this lesson's key verse means in your life.**

6) **What was Caiaphas saying in verses 49–50, and why was it so ironic?**

7) **This chapter brings Jesus' general ministry to a close. In the next chapter, the events of His final week begin to unfold. How has your relationship with Jesus been affected by this study to this point?**

Humble Encounters and Grand Entrances

What is the proper way for a king to present himself to his people? If Jesus is king, how do we meet Him? Everyone has preconceived ideas. They usually include pomp and circumstance. But Jesus came riding on a donkey's colt. Why? And whom did He meet along the way?

John 12:1–50

Mary Anoints Jesus at Bethany

12 Six days before the Passover, Jesus therefore came to Bethany, where Lazarus was, whom Jesus had raised from the dead. [2]So they gave a dinner for him there. Martha served, and Lazarus was one of those reclining with him at the table. [3]Mary therefore took a pound of expensive ointment made from pure nard, and anointed the feet of Jesus and wiped his feet with her hair. The house was filled with the fragrance of the perfume. [4]But Judas Iscariot, one of his disciples (he who was about to betray him), said, [5]"Why was this ointment not sold for three hundred denarii and given to the poor?" [6]He said this, not because he cared about the poor, but because he was a thief, and having charge of the moneybag he used to help himself to what was put into it. [7]Jesus said, "Leave her alone, so that she may keep it for the day of my burial. [8]The poor you always have with you, but you do not always have me."

The Plot to Kill Lazarus

[9]When the large crowd of the Jews learned that Jesus was there, they came, not only on account of him but also to see Lazarus, whom he had raised from the dead. [10]So the chief priests made plans to put Lazarus to death as well, [11]because on account of him many of the Jews were going away and believing in Jesus.

The Triumphal Entry

[12]The next day the large crowd that had come to the feast heard that Jesus was coming to Jerusalem. [13]So they took branches of palm trees and went out to meet him, crying out, "Hosanna! Blessed is he who comes in the name of the Lord, even the King of Israel!" [14]And Jesus found a young donkey and sat on it, just as it is written,

[15]Fear not, daughter of Zion;

behold, your king is coming,

sitting on a donkey's colt!"

[16]His disciples did not understand these things at first, but when Jesus was glorified, then they remembered that these things had been written about him and had been done to him. [17]The crowd that had been with him when he called Lazarus out of the tomb and raised him from the dead continued to bear witness. [18]The reason why the crowd went to meet him was that they heard he had done this sign. [19]So the Pharisees said to one another, "You see that you are gaining nothing. Look, the world has gone after him."

Key Verse

"Truly, truly, I say to you, unless a grain of wheat falls into the earth and dies, it remains alone; but if it dies, it bears much fruit" (John 12:24).

Some Greeks Seek Jesus

[20]Now among those who went up to worship at the feast were some Greeks. [21]So these came to Philip, who was from Bethsaida in Galilee, and asked him, "Sir, we wish to see Jesus." [22]Philip went and told Andrew; Andrew and Philip went and told Jesus. [23]And Jesus answered them, "The hour has come for the Son of Man to

be glorified. ²⁴Truly, truly, I say to you, unless a grain of wheat falls into the earth and dies, it remains alone; but if it dies, it bears much fruit. ²⁵Whoever loves his life loses it, and whoever hates his life in this world will keep it for eternal life. ²⁶If anyone serves me, he must follow me; and where I am, there will my servant be also. If anyone serves me, the Father will honor him.

The Son of Man Must Be Lifted Up

²⁷"Now is my soul troubled. And what shall I say? 'Father, save me from this hour'? But for this purpose I have come to this hour. ²⁸Father, glorify your name." Then a voice came from heaven: "I have glorified it, and I will glorify it again." ²⁹The crowd that stood there and heard it said that it had thundered. Others said, "An angel has spoken to him." ³⁰Jesus answered, "This voice has come for your sake, not mine. ³¹Now is the judgment of this world; now will the ruler of this world be cast out. ³²And I, when I am lifted up from the earth, will draw all people to myself." ³³He said this to show by what kind of death he was going to die. ³⁴So the crowd answered him, "We have heard from the Law that the Christ remains forever. How can you say that the Son of Man must be lifted up? Who is this Son of Man?" ³⁵So Jesus said to them, "The light is among you for a little while longer. Walk while you have the light, lest darkness overtake you. The one who walks in the darkness does not know where he is going. ³⁶While you have the light, believe in the light, that you may become sons of light."

The Unbelief of the People

When Jesus had said these things, he departed and hid himself from them. ³⁷Though he had done so many signs before them, they still did not believe in him, ³⁸so that the word spoken by the prophet Isaiah might be fulfilled:

"Lord, who has believed what he heard from us,

and to whom has the arm of the Lord been revealed?"

³⁹Therefore they could not believe. For again Isaiah said,

⁴⁰"He has blinded their eyes

and hardened their heart,

lest they see with their eyes,

and understand with their heart, and turn,

and I would heal them."

⁴¹Isaiah said these things because he saw his glory and spoke of him. ⁴²Nevertheless, many even of the authorities believed in him, but for fear of the Pharisees they did not confess it, so that they would not be put out of the synagogue; ⁴³for they loved the glory that comes from man more than the glory that comes from God.

Jesus Came to Save the World

⁴⁴And Jesus cried out and said, "Whoever believes in me, believes not in me but in him who sent me. ⁴⁵And whoever sees me sees him who sent me. ⁴⁶I have come into the world as light, so that whoever believes in me may not remain in darkness. ⁴⁷If anyone hears my words and does not keep them, I do not judge him; for I did not come to judge the world but to save the world. ⁴⁸The one who rejects me and does not receive my words has a judge; the word that I have spoken will judge him on the last day. ⁴⁹For I have not spoken on my own authority, but the Father who sent me has himself given me a commandment—what to say and what to speak. ⁵⁰And I know that his commandment is eternal life. What I say, therefore, I say as the Father has told me."

Go Deeper

Jesus stunned the crowd when He said, "And I, when I am lifted up from the earth, will draw all people to myself" (John 12:32). His hearers understood Jesus' phrase "lifted up" to mean His death. But they couldn't square that with their understanding of the Messiah. They assumed that passages like Psalm 89:4,36–37; Isaiah 9:7 and Ezekiel 37:25 referred to a coming Christ who "remains forever." These passages referred to the eternal nature of God's promises to David and were fulfilled in Jesus, but not in the way people expected. He is the eternal Savior, and His death did not nullify His special role, because His Resurrection put death in proper context. Death is not the end of things, only part of the story.

Historically, Jesus' phrase referred directly to an event that occurred during the wilderness wanderings of Israel. The sins of the people led to a plague of vipers whose bites killed. When they repented, God had Moses raise the likeness of a serpent, and those who looked at it, trusting in God, survived. (See Num. 21:4–9.) It is one of many Old Testament examples of how God built into people's experiences the means to understand Jesus' work on the cross.

Tensions were near a boiling point. Interest and intrigue swirled around Jesus as people flocked to see Him, meet Him, touch and greet Him. Feverish plans were also underway to destroy Jesus.

Something had to "give." He had a wide, if shallow, popular support, but the hatred and intentions of His opponents ran deep. He was definitely the added attraction in Jerusalem during Passover that year. Little did even those intimately involved understand that there would never again be a Passover quite like the one they were about to experience.

Chapter 12 of John offers a panoramic view of various encounters Jesus had during those turbulent days. Among these were personal moments with Mary and with Judas Iscariot. Then came the spontaneous outpouring of praise from the pilgrim crowd on its way to Jerusalem, creating what we call the Triumphal Entry.

The disciples were as clueless about the meaning of these events as the crowd. (See John 12:16.) The Pharisees came among the crowds to meet Jesus, driven by fear, envy and what we could now call "informed misunderstanding." They had the best preparation for grasping who Jesus was, but they couldn't see beyond their personal bias and positions of prestige. Strangers also came to meet Jesus. A group of Greeks identified Philip as the disciple with the Greek name and asked him to introduce them to Jesus.

Faced with all this attention, Jesus stunned the seekers with ominous words: "Unless a grain of wheat falls into the earth and dies. ... Whoever loves his life loses it" (12:24–25). These words must have troubled many, including His disciples, who thought Jesus was well on His way to the crown and the throne. Instead, He was on His way to a crown of thorns and a cross. It would have been natural for the crowd to conclude that when Jesus said, "The hour has come for the Son of Man to be glorified" (v. 23), He meant that He was ready to take His position as the new king of Israel, the Messiah, who would lead them out from under the tyranny of the Romans.

But the glory of the throne and an earthly kingdom paled before Jesus' vision of His true purpose—to establish an eternal kingdom filled with citizens who were Spirit-born. But He also knew what that kingdom would cost Him. "Looking to Jesus, the founder and perfecter of our faith, who for the joy that was set before him endured the cross, despising the shame, and is seated at the right hand of the throne of God" (Heb. 12:2).

Two people in this chapter met Jesus in a way worth imitating. The encounter occurred on the night before the Triumphal Entry. Jesus and His disciples were probably staying with newly raised Lazarus and his sisters. That evening, Martha catered a special dinner to honor Jesus. This time, instead of sitting at Jesus' feet as she had done in the past (see Luke 10:38–42), Mary carefully chose her own way of expressing gratitude to Jesus. Each of these sisters had learned a valuable lesson from the Lord. Martha had learned to serve quietly and humbly. She didn't demand that Mary "get busy." Mary, for her part, learned to add an action component to her devotion to Jesus.

As was the custom of the time, the men actually reclined

> **"** *The glory of the throne and an earthly kingdom paled before Jesus' vision of His true purpose.* **"**

around the low table as they ate. Mary knelt at Jesus' feet, drenched them with costly perfume and then wiped them with her long hair. Apparently, she said nothing. She let her actions speak louder than words. But others, including Judas, voiced their objections. Was she not wasting a precious commodity that could be used to help the poor? How easy it is to question and devalue another's effort! John couldn't help but note the irony that Judas would look down on Mary when he was guilty of dipping into the disciples' moneybag for his own purposes.

Jesus accepted Mary's gesture as an appropriate way to prepare for His death. She may not have had that specific end in mind, but her simple, costly honor moved Jesus deeply. She and her sister, without fanfare, gave Jesus an encouraging reminder that all He was about to endure would bear fruit.

The lavish show that came the next morning, punctuated by the tears in Jesus' eyes as He looked over Jerusalem, launched Holy Week. How appropriate that the rich fragrance from Mary's gift prepared the Lord for the long way He would travel on His journey to the cross!

Express It

As you pray, thank God for accepting your actions of sacrificial worship. Pray that others will be affected by the "fragrance" of your life, not to bring attention to you, but to bring attention to Christ. Ask Him to help you identify ways you can "waste what is costly" in service for Him, including what you might do for the poor.

Consider It

As you read John 12:1–50, consider these questions:

1) How do you work out the tension between honoring Christ and caring for the poor?

_____

_____

_____

_____

2) What stands out for you about John's description of the Triumphal Entry?

_____

_____

_____

_____

3) In what ways do you regularly meet Jesus? How do you prepare?

_____

_____

_____

_____

4) How would you explain Jesus' response to the Greek seekers in verses 24–26?

_____

_____

_____

_____

5) What indications do you see in this chapter about Jesus' state of mind?

_____

_____

_____

_____

6) Why were some of those who did believe in Jesus afraid to make their faith public? How does this parallel our hesitation today?

_____

_____

_____

The Master Servant

The aroma of roast lamb had everyone practically drooling. Thirteen hungry men crowded into an upper room and jostled for a place at the table. No one wanted to hold up the proceedings. It was time to eat. Then Jesus got up from the table and began to do what someone else should have volunteered to do.

John 13:1–38

Jesus Washes the Disciples' Feet

13 Now before the Feast of the Passover, when Jesus knew that his hour had come to depart out of this world to the Father, having loved his own who were in the world, he loved them to the end. ²During supper, when the devil had already put it into the heart of Judas Iscariot, Simon's son, to betray him, ³Jesus, knowing that the Father had given all things into his hands, and that he had come from God and was going back to God, ⁴rose from supper. He laid aside his outer garments, and taking a towel, tied it around his waist. ⁵Then he poured water into a basin and began to wash the disciples' feet and to wipe them with the towel that was wrapped around him. ⁶He came to Simon Peter, who said to him, "Lord, do you wash my feet?" ⁷Jesus answered him, "What I am doing you do not understand now, but afterward you will understand." ⁸Peter said to him, "You shall never wash my feet." Jesus answered him, "If I do not wash you, you have no share with me." ⁹Simon Peter said to him, "Lord, not my feet only but also my hands and my head!" ¹⁰Jesus said to him, "The one who has bathed does not need to wash, except for his feet, but is completely clean. And you are clean, but not every one of you." ¹¹For he knew who was to betray him; that was why he said, "Not all of you are clean."

¹²When he had washed their feet and put on his outer garments and resumed his place, he said to them, "Do you understand what I have done to you? ¹³You call me Teacher and Lord, and you are right, for so I am. ¹⁴If I then, your Lord and Teacher, have washed your feet, you also ought to wash one another's feet. ¹⁵For I have given you an example, that you also should do just as I have done to you. ¹⁶Truly, truly, I say to you, a servant is not greater than his master, nor is a messenger greater than

the one who sent him. ¹⁷If you know these things, blessed are you if you do them. ¹⁸I am not speaking of all of you; I know whom I have chosen. But the Scripture will be fulfilled, 'He who ate my bread has lifted his heel against me.' ¹⁹I am telling you this now, before it takes place, that when it does take place you may believe that I am he. ²⁰Truly, truly, I say to you, whoever receives the one I send receives me, and whoever receives me receives the one who sent me."

Key Verse

"A new commandment I give to you, that you love one another: just as I have loved you, you also are to love one another" (John 13:34).

One of You Will Betray Me

²¹After saying these things, Jesus was troubled in his spirit, and testified, "Truly, truly, I say to you, one of you will betray me." ²²The disciples looked at one another, uncertain of whom he spoke. ²³One of his disciples, whom Jesus loved, was reclining at table close to Jesus, ²⁴so Simon Peter motioned to him to ask Jesus of whom he was speaking. ²⁵So that disciple, leaning back against Jesus, said to him, "Lord, who is it?" ²⁶Jesus answered, "It is he to whom I will give this morsel of bread when I have dipped it." So when he had dipped the morsel, he gave it to Judas, the son of Simon Iscariot. ²⁷Then after he had taken the morsel, Satan entered into him.

Jesus said to him, "What you are going to do, do quickly." [28]Now no one at the table knew why he said this to him. [29]Some thought that, because Judas had the moneybag, Jesus was telling him, "Buy what we need for the feast," or that he should give something to the poor. [30]So, after receiving the morsel of bread, he immediately went out. And it was night.

A New Commandment

[31]When he had gone out, Jesus said, "Now is the Son of Man glorified, and God is glorified in him. [32]If God is glorified in him, God will also glorify him in himself, and glorify him at once. [33]Little children, yet a little while I am with you. You will seek me, and just as I said to the Jews, so now I also say to you, 'Where I am going you cannot come.' [34]A new commandment I give to you, that you love one another: just as I have loved you, you also are to love one another. [35]By this all people will know that you are my disciples, if you have love for one another."

Jesus Foretells Peter's Denial

[36]Simon Peter said to him, "Lord, where are you going?" Jesus answered him, "Where I am going you cannot follow me now, but you will follow afterward." [37]Peter said to him, "Lord, why can I not follow you now? I will lay down my life for you." [38]Jesus answered, "Will you lay down your life for me? Truly, truly, I say to you, the rooster will not crow till you have denied me three times."

Go Deeper

Someone wisely and sadly remarked that the best way to discover what a servant feels like is to have someone treat you like one. But the truth is that service will often be overlooked. Jesus Himself described the reality of service in Luke 17:7–10. On this side of eternity we should not engage in service expecting to be recognized. It may happen, but recognition should not be our motivation.

Interestingly enough, the words Jesus has invited us to expect from Him when we arrive in eternity have to do with service: "His master said to him, 'Well done, good and faithful servant. You have been faithful over a little; I will set you over much. Enter into the joy of your master'" (Matt. 25:21). That hope offers us a powerful motivation.

Another motivation to serve comes from recognizing how much we have been served. We serve others, not because *they* will be grateful but because *we are grateful* for all that Christ has done for us. We obey and please Jesus when we serve those He loves—our friends and family. One of the best ways you can express your gratitude to Jesus today is by finding someone to serve with a smile.

We don't expect certain people to do mundane tasks. We sense something odd and even uncomfortable when we see someone we admire having to undertake a duty someone else should have joyfully done for them. Watching an elderly person lift a heavy suitcase or an important leader hanging coats at a dinner given in his honor immediately raises questions. Why isn't someone else doing that? Won't somebody help? Who's not doing their job?

In Jesus' day, foot washing was a practical necessity. Open footwear and dusty roads made for dirty feet. Combined with the constant presence of animals on the pathways and the common practice of using the streets for sewage disposal, the circumstances emphasized the importance of clean feet. Household servants typically took care of this detail.

Enter the disciples. Their track record for helping each other was dismal. They were much more likely to argue over who was greatest than to see the opportunity to wash each others' feet. A couple of the disciples had already done "their share" in overseeing the preparation of the meal. The rest were too hungry to even notice such a detail.

Jesus looked at that motley crew of His followers and loved them. He didn't berate or rebuke them. He stood and wrapped a towel around His waist. Then the One before whom people regularly bowed in worship bent His knees in a messy ministry of cleansing filthy feet. The disciples were shocked and shamed. Peter couldn't bear the humiliation. He tried to prevent Jesus from washing his feet. But Jesus wasn't about to accept offended pride or belated shame. He was giving a priceless lesson in love and service. When He was finished, Jesus put on His cloak and sat down. It's probably worth noting that the disciples still didn't "get it." Not a single one of them leaped to wash Jesus' feet.

Jesus addressed their lack of camaraderie by making the point, "If I then, your Lord and Teacher, have washed your feet, you also ought to wash one another's feet" (John 13:14). In a sense, Jesus began the final leg of His journey to the cross on His knees, washing toes and calluses.

The time was drawing near. Judas' guarded eyes couldn't hide the intent of his heart from the Master. Jesus had a lot to tell His disciples, and Judas was in no mood to listen. So, Jesus mentioned again that a betrayer was among His inner circle. Then He sent Judas out without a confrontation, knowing that His Father was ultimately in charge of the events that would fill the next hours with suffering. The sound of Judas' departing footsteps had hardly faded when Jesus said, "A new commandment I give to you, that you love one another: just as I have loved you, you also are to love one another" (13:34).

Why was the new commandment new? Because Jesus expressed the ancient command of God in Leviticus 19:18 in a new way. It wasn't new as if He had just invented it; it was new as He had just illustrated it. It is new as He would perfectly illustrate it on the cross the next day. It would remain new as each succeeding generation of His followers discovered that the world is watching to see how we treat each other.

Jesus pointed out how high the stakes are when He added, "By this all people will know that you are my disciples, if you have love for one another" (John 13:35). Jesus did not say it is through the purity of our theology, through the understanding we have of God's Word, that we will make a difference in the world. Rather it is through our love for one another that the world will know we are Christians.

This command to love one another echoes in the background of everything else Jesus said during those moments in the upper room. The Holy Spirit whom Jesus promised has as one of His

> *"Jesus did not say it is through the purity of our theology, through the understanding we have of God's Word, that we will make a difference in the world. Rather it is through our love for one another that the world will know we are Christians."*

primary roles to assist us as we love each other. The next four chapters record those final lessons Jesus passed on to His disciples before the turbulent hours of His arrest, trial and crucifixion. Because we know the outcome, we have every reason to pay close attention to these words of Christ.

Express It

What Jesus made a big deal about in practice, we ought to begin to make a big deal about in prayer. How can we more readily recognize opportunities for service? We can ask the Lord to help us see others the way He sees them. When we ask God to help us love others better, He will always answer by giving us opportunities to serve them better.

Consider It

As you read John 13:1–38, consider these questions:

1) Washing feet was about as common a routine in ancient times as washing hands before eating is today. Why did the disciples forget?

2) Foot washing is not widely practiced today, but what acts of service most represent this kind of gesture for you?

3) Was Jesus motivated to teach or to love? Why?

4) How did Jesus' actions set the mood for the entire meal?

5) In what ways did Jesus demonstrate His love for Judas on this occasion?

6) What connection do you see between verse 33, "Where I am going you cannot come," and verse 34, "Love one another"?

7) Why did Jesus tell Peter about the disciple's denial (vv. 36–38)?

8) What difference does it make that Jesus already knows the ways in which you will fail today and tomorrow?

Lesson

14

The Truth for Troubled Hearts

Christianity is the most exclusive religion in the world. It not only claims to offer ultimate truth but points to Jesus as the embodiment of that truth. As long as it insists that Jesus is the only way to God, Christianity has to be exclusive. But can it survive in this pluralistic world? Does it still have a message every human must ultimately accept or reject?

John 14:1–31

I Am the Way, and the Truth, and the Life

14 "Let not your hearts be troubled. Believe in God; believe also in me. [2]In my Father's house are many rooms. If it were not so, would I have told you that I go to prepare a place for you? [3]And if I go and prepare a place for you, I will come again and will take you to myself, that where I am you may be also. [4]And you know the way to where I am going." [5]Thomas said to him, "Lord, we do not know where you are going. How can we know the way?" [6]Jesus said to him, "I am the way, and the truth, and the life. No one comes to the Father except through me. [7]If you had known me, you would have known my Father also. From now on you do know him and have seen him."

[8]Philip said to him, "Lord, show us the Father, and it is enough for us." [9]Jesus said to him, "Have I been with you so long, and you still do not know me, Philip? Whoever has seen me has seen the Father. How can you say, 'Show us the Father'? [10]Do you not believe that I am in the Father and the Father is in me? The words that I say to you I do not speak on my own authority, but the Father who dwells in me does his works. [11]Believe me that I am in the Father and the Father is in me, or else believe on account of the works themselves.

[12]"Truly, truly, I say to you, whoever believes in me will also do the works that I do; and greater works than these will he do, because I am going to the Father. [13]Whatever you ask in my name, this I will do, that the Father may be glorified in the Son. [14]If you ask me anything in my name, I will do it.

Jesus Promises the Holy Spirit

[15]"If you love me, you will keep my commandments. [16]And I will ask the Father, and he will give you another Helper, to be with you forever, [17]even the Spirit of truth,

> # Key Verse
> *Jesus said to him, "I am the way, and the truth, and the life. No one comes to the Father except through me"* (John 14:6).

whom the world cannot receive, because it neither sees him nor knows him. You know him, for he dwells with you and will be in you.

[18]"I will not leave you as orphans; I will come to you. [19]Yet a little while and the world will see me no more, but you will see me. Because I live, you also will live. [20]In that day you will know that I am in my Father, and you in me, and I in you. [21]Whoever has my commandments and keeps them, he it is who loves me. And he who loves me will be loved by my Father, and I will love him and manifest myself to him." [22]Judas (not Iscariot) said to him, "Lord, how is it that you will manifest yourself to us, and not to the world?" [23]Jesus answered him, "If anyone loves me, he will keep my word, and my Father will love him,

and we will come to him and make our home with him. ²⁴Whoever does not love me does not keep my words. And the word that you hear is not mine but the Father's who sent me.

²⁵"These things I have spoken to you while I am still with you. ²⁶But the Helper, the Holy Spirit, whom the Father will send in my name, he will teach you all things and bring to your remembrance all that I have said to you. ²⁷Peace I leave with you; my peace I give to you. Not as the world gives do I give to you. Let not your hearts be troubled, neither let them be afraid. ²⁸You heard me say to you, 'I am going away, and I will come to you.' If you loved me, you would have rejoiced, because I am going to the Father, for the Father is greater than I. ²⁹And now I have told you before it takes place, so that when it does take place you may believe. ³⁰I will no longer talk much with you, for the ruler of this world is coming. He has no claim on me, ³¹but I do as the Father has commanded me, so that the world may know that I love the Father. Rise, let us go from here."

Go Deeper

Jesus mentioned the Holy Spirit in the three central chapters that record His words during the Last Supper in the Gospel of John (John 14:16,26; 15:26; 16:7). The term "helper" translates a Greek word that has also been rendered "advocate," "counselor" or "comforter." The Old Testament mentioned the Holy Spirit as God's empowering presence in people's lives for certain tasks or purposes. (See Ex. 31:2–6; Judg. 15:14–15; Isa. 11:2.)

Jesus promised the Holy Spirit as the indwelling, instructing and guiding presence of God in the lives of those who love Jesus and keep His commandments (John 14:15). Passages like John 14:26, "But the Helper, the Holy Spirit, whom the Father will send in my name, he will teach you all things and bring to your remembrance all that I have said to you," make it clear that the Holy Spirit is an equal and active member of the Trinity.

The underlying comfort of John 14 has to do with the focus on two homes. The first is the Father's house, the destination of those who trust in Jesus as the way, the truth and the life. But the second home is an immediate dwelling place in us where God abides when we trust in Christ (v. 23). Before we get to the Father's house, we get to *be* the dwelling place for the Father, Son and Holy Spirit. How great is that!

Even people who don't particularly believe in heaven find it attractive to think of death as "going home." Wouldn't it be nice if there were a heaven and it turned out to be a big, wonderful house with lots of rooms where we could all live together? They are delighted and amazed when they read Jesus' words at the beginning of John 14: "Let not your hearts be troubled. Believe in God; believe also in me. In my Father's house are many rooms. If it were not so, would I have told you that I go to prepare a place for you?" (vv. 1–2).

This sounds good in modern ears—at least the house part. But modern minds take this picture and conclude that Jesus also meant that along with the "many rooms" came many doorways. We can hardly imagine a house with one entrance, so we conclude that God must have provided multiple doors. It seems only right that each of us gets to choose whatever door suits us.

That is, until we get to verse 6, when Jesus flatly calls Himself "*the* way, *the* truth and *the* life" (emphasis added) and concludes, "No one comes to the Father except through me." The exclusiveness of Christianity comes from statements Jesus made like these. He told us death can be like going home, but there's only one way to get there. That way leads through Him and only through Him.

If this sounds unfair and unreasonable, you are hearing it with a pluralistic mind. The pluralistic mind (one that thinks there are many answers to every question) has a hard time making itself up. In fact, pluralism hates decisions, because a decision involves choosing an answer and excluding others. Pluralism tries to look at life and eternity like a map. It says, "See, there are many roads to get from point A to point B. One is as good as another." This discussion only works as long as you are simply looking at a map. As soon as you begin to drive, you will have to choose which road you will take. When you decide which road to take, you have excluded all others.

Pluralism is actually a way to sound fair while avoiding important decisions. Saying "I believe there are many ways to get into heaven" is like saying there are many doorways into a house. But if you actually want to get into the house, you are going to have to choose one door. Jesus said, "I'm the door to choose because I'm the only one." This means that people can choose other doors or no door, but none of those choices will get them into the Father's house.

Jesus made it impossible for us to believe in Him as one of many ways to get to the Father. He is *the* Way or no way at all. People can and do choose other ways to try to get to heaven all the time. If Jesus was right, none of them will make it. If Jesus was wrong, then we can't get to heaven through Him either. If we try to say that we believe in Jesus as *our* way into heaven but others can find other ways to get into heaven, we are not telling the truth. We are admitting we don't believe in one of Jesus' central claims—that He is the only way.

If we read the Last Supper passage in John 13–17, the troubled hearts of chapter 14 will probably not surprise us. Jesus had given the humbling footwashing lesson followed by crushing news that someone would betray Him and the challenge that they were to love one another in His absence. The disciples were experiencing the original version of a problem that still plagues us today: How do we follow someone whom we can't see and touch? How do we trust Someone who's out of sight? Somehow their troubled hearts seem a lot like ours.

That's why Jesus reminded us that He is the way, the truth and the life for troubled hearts. That's why He promised the Holy Spirit. That's why He assured the disciples and us that His physical absence doesn't mean He isn't with us. We can't see Him, and we may not be able to "feel" His presence all the time, but we trust His promise to be with us without interruption.

"Jesus made it impossible for us to believe in Him as one of many ways to get to the Father. He is the Way or no way at all."

When we want the peace the world tries to offer (feeling good inside for a few moments), Jesus speaks the truth for troubled hearts: "Peace I leave with you; my peace I give to you. Not as the world gives do I give to you. Let not your hearts be troubled, neither let them be afraid" (14:27).

Express It

What's the level of "trouble" in your heart today? Jesus' presence in your life doesn't mean an absence of trouble. (See John 16:33.) Jesus tells us to expect trouble. Our awareness of trouble reminds us not only to focus on our trust in God and His Son but also to turn over those things that trouble us to Him. What "troubling" matters can you deliberately hand over to God in prayer today?

Consider It

As you read John 14:1–31, consider these questions:

1) How did the disciples reveal the depth of their troubled hearts?

_____

_____

_____

2) What did Jesus teach in this chapter about His relationship to the Father?

_____

_____

_____

3) Describe what you have learned about Jesus' role as "the way," "the truth" and "the life."

_____

_____

_____

4) How did Jesus describe the role of the Holy Spirit in this chapter?

_____

_____

_____

5) Why did Jesus say the disciples should be glad over His departure (v. 28)?

_____

_____

_____

6) How does the world try to offer us peace? Why does it always fail?

_____

_____

_____

7) How would you describe the peace you have experienced in Christ?

_____

_____

_____

On the Vine

What do you need in order to stay alive? Most of us can't last more than a few minutes without air. We require water in order to function. Some of us even think we can't last without food for more than a few hours. And, no, chocolate really shouldn't be on the list of life's essentials. But, as we'll see in this lesson, there's a need deeper and stronger than all of these that determines life.

John 15:1–27

I Am the True Vine

15 "I am the true vine, and my Father is the vinedresser. ²Every branch of mine that does not bear fruit he takes away, and every branch that does bear fruit he prunes, that it may bear more fruit. ³Already you are clean because of the word that I have spoken to you. ⁴Abide in me, and I in you. As the branch cannot bear fruit by itself, unless it abides in the vine, neither can you, unless you abide in me. ⁵I am the vine; you are the branches. Whoever abides in me and I in him, he it is that bears much fruit, for apart from me you can do nothing. ⁶If anyone does not abide in me he is thrown away like a branch and withers; and the branches are gathered, thrown into the fire, and burned. ⁷If you abide in me, and my words abide in you, ask whatever you wish, and it will be done for you. ⁸By this my Father is glorified, that you bear much fruit and so prove to be my disciples. ⁹As the Father has loved me, so have I loved you. Abide in my love. ¹⁰If you keep my commandments, you will abide in my love, just as I have kept my Father's commandments and abide in his love. ¹¹These things I have spoken to you, that my joy may be in you, and that your joy may be full.

> # Key Verse
>
> *"You did not choose me, but I chose you and appointed you that you should go and bear fruit and that your fruit should abide, so that whatever you ask the Father in my name, he may give it to you"* (John 15:16).

¹²"This is my commandment, that you love one another as I have loved you. ¹³Greater love has no one than this, that someone lays down his life for his friends. ¹⁴You are my friends if you do what I command you. ¹⁵No longer do I call you servants, for the servant does not know what his master is doing; but I have called you friends, for all that I have heard from my Father I have made known to you. ¹⁶You did not choose me, but I chose you and appointed you that you should go and bear fruit and that your fruit should abide, so that whatever you ask the Father in my name, he may give it to you. ¹⁷These things I command you, so that you will love one another.

The Hatred of the World

¹⁸"If the world hates you, know that it has hated me before it hated you. ¹⁹If you were of the world, the world would love you as its own; but because you are not of the world, but I chose you out of the world, therefore the world hates you. ²⁰Remember the word that I said to you: 'A servant is not greater than his master.' If they persecuted me, they will also persecute you. If they kept my word, they will also keep yours. ²¹But all these things they will do to you on account of my name, because they do not know him who sent me. ²²If I had not come and spoken to them, they would not have been guilty of sin, but now they have no excuse for their sin. ²³Whoever hates me hates my Father also. ²⁴If I had not done among them the works that no one else did, they would not be guilty of sin, but now they have seen and hated both me and my Father. ²⁵But the word that is written in their Law must be fulfilled: 'They hated me without a cause.'

²⁶"But when the Helper comes, whom I will send to you from the Father, the Spirit of truth, who proceeds from the Father, he will bear witness about me. ²⁷And you also will bear witness, because you have been with me from the beginning."

Go Deeper

Jesus said, "You are my friends if you do what I command you" (John 15:14). So, why is Jesus your friend? Because He loves you (15:12). When does He call you His friend? When you are obedient—when you do what He asks. So, what is Jesus to you when you are disobedient?

This question forces us to examine how we often think about relationships. Jesus doesn't cease to be our friend when we fail. We don't earn His friendship or forgiveness. Both are given freely. His love and grace have been directed toward us even before we sinned or failed. (See Rom. 5:8.) Our friendship with Christ may be shamefully erratic; His friendship toward us is pow-

erful, constant and truthful. He doesn't threaten to stop loving us as a way of controlling us. His love simply draws us back from sin.

As if to underscore this point, Jesus said, "You did not choose me, but I chose you and appointed you that you should go and bear fruit and that your fruit should abide, so that whatever you ask the Father in my name, he may give it to you" (John 15:16). Jesus chose us to bear fruit, not the other way around. We don't bear fruit in order to be chosen or accepted. We want to bear fruit out of deep gratitude for having been chosen.

Jesus is the life-giver. By this point in John's Gospel, we've learned that Jesus can supply "living water" (4:10, 7:38). He claimed to be "the life" (14:6), the "bread of life" (6:35), the source of words about eternal life (6:68) and the only access to eternal life (3:16, 14:6).

During the Last Supper, Jesus gave His disciples an unforgettable picture of the relationship He wants to have with us. He described our dependence on Him as the same as the dependence of branches to their vine. Jesus is the vine; we're the branches; never the other way around. Life only flows one way—from Him to us.

Just because we can't see the connection between two objects doesn't mean it doesn't exist. The plastic stick full of buttons seems a little pointless, until we press one button and the TV turns on. Our car keys now have buttons that lock and unlock our doors and even beep our horns and flash headlights when we forget where we parked! Many appliances now come with voice activation. The connections are invisible but real. The connections between Jesus, the Vine, and us, the branches, are just as unseen but just as real.

Today's amazing cell-phone technology takes "connection" to a whole new level! There's probably never been a time in history when more people were affected by competing connections. How often have you had an important conversation interrupted by a ringing cell phone? Some of us even allow our phone conversations to be interrupted by other phone calls. It seems as if we're connected to everyone all the time and at any time.

Why would we give others so much access to our lives? Perhaps we have come to believe that any connection is better than no connection at all. When does our total connection with the rest of the world become a distraction? When we don't choose wisely between competing connections. When we can't bear to turn off our cell phones for a while because we're afraid that among all those not-so-important calls might be one we don't want to miss. But we often fail to notice that our anxiety for connection with others competes with a connection we can't afford to take for granted. How many numbers could be taken off our speed-dial list if we could replace them with Jesus' number?

We who follow Jesus in this age of multiple connections can't forget what He meant by "I am the vine; you are the branches" (15:5). We don't want our connection with Jesus to be like the "potential connection" between the tower and a cell phone that has been turned off. We want our connection to be active. So, what does this involve?

Jesus used a word to describe the vine-branch bond that has often been translated "abide" or "remain." "Abide in me and I in you" (v. 4). Jesus used the word ten times in the first ten verses of this chapter. It refers to the kind of vital connection through which life, strength and spiritual health flows. This connection yields fruit. Fruit comes about as a result of two benefits Jesus provides: His words (v. 7) and His love (v. 10). The absolute

> **"**_Jesus is the vine; we're the branches;_
> _never the other way around. Life only_
> _flows one way—from Him to us._**"**

Lordship of Jesus is expressed as we abide in Him and His love and His words abide in us.

As our lives are filled and guided by His words and His love, fruit such as the fruit of the Spirit (Gal. 5:22) naturally develops in its season. This fruit (love, joy, peace, etc.) is desirable to us but often not produced in our lives because we are not "abiding." We're trying to live as disconnected, independent branches (with our cell phones turned off) while expecting to experience the results that only come when we are living in Christ and He is living in us.

One great way to begin each day is to ask Christ to help you draw on your spiritual attachment to Him so that His life can flow through your connection. That's a request He loves to answer. After all, Jesus is the life-giver!

Express It

As you pray, consider the final challenge in this lesson's devotional. Have you lived today more as someone attached to Jesus or someone with a live connection with Him? Think of Jesus being like the guy on the cell phone commercial who keeps saying, "Can you hear me now?" Express your desire to be someone with clear reception of what Jesus wants to say to you.

Consider It

As you read John 15:1–27, consider these questions:

1) How do the opening verses of this chapter describe the way Jesus and God the Father function in dealing with people?

_____

_____

_____

2) In what ways do the experiences of those who abide in the vine differ from those who don't?

_____

_____

_____

3) How did Jesus explain His use of the word "friends" to describe His disciples?

_____

_____

_____

4) In the context of Jesus' words here, what is fruit?

_____

_____

_____

5) When Jesus speaks of the world's hatred (vv.18–27), to what is He referring?

_____

_____

_____

6) Each section of this chapter (1–17 and 18–27) compares two groups of people. Is Jesus giving two versions of the same comparison or talking about two different subjects?

_____

_____

_____

7) In what sense are you abiding in Christ as you move through your day today?

_____

_____

_____

Lesson 16

The Constant Counselor

In the last lesson, we compared our connection to Jesus with the connections available through cell phones. Most cells phones include a GPS unit (Global Positioning System) that continuously monitors the phone's location. In this lesson, we'll discuss the GPS unit that God places in us— God's Present Spirit. What does the Holy Spirit do in our lives?

16 "I have said all these things to you to keep you from falling away. ²They will put you out of the synagogues. Indeed, the hour is coming when whoever kills you will think he is offering service to God. ³And they will do these things because they have not known the Father, nor me. ⁴But I have said these things to you, that when their hour comes you may remember that I told them to you.

The Work of the Holy Spirit

"I did not say these things to you from the beginning, because I was with you. ⁵But now I am going to him who sent me, and none of you asks me, 'Where are you going?' ⁶But because I have said these things to you, sorrow has filled your heart. ⁷Nevertheless, I tell you the truth: it is to your advantage that I go away, for if I do not go away, the Helper will not come to you. But if I go, I will send him to you. ⁸And when he comes, he will convict the world concerning sin and righteousness and judgment: ⁹concerning sin, because they do not believe in me; ¹⁰concerning righteousness, because I go to the Father, and you will see me no longer; ¹¹concerning judgment, because the ruler of this world is judged.

¹²"I still have many things to say to you, but you cannot bear them now. ¹³When the Spirit of truth comes, he will guide you into all the truth, for he will not speak on his own authority, but whatever he hears he will speak, and he will declare to you the things that are to come. ¹⁴He will glorify me, for he will take what is mine and declare it to you. ¹⁵All that the Father has is mine; therefore I said that he will take what is mine and declare it to you.

Key Verse

"When the Spirit of truth comes, he will guide you into all the truth, for he will not speak on his own authority, but whatever he hears he will speak, and he will declare to you the things that are to come" (John 16:13).

Your Sorrow Will Turn into Joy

¹⁶"A little while, and you will see me no longer; and again a little while, and you will see me." ¹⁷So some of his disciples said to one another, "What is this that he says to us, 'A little while, and you will not see me, and again a little while, and you will see me'; and, 'because I am going to the Father'?" ¹⁸So they were saying, "What does he mean by 'a little while'? We do not know what he is talking about." ¹⁹Jesus knew that they wanted to ask him, so he said to them, "Is this what you are asking yourselves, what I meant by saying, 'A little while and you will not see me, and again a little while and you will see me'? ²⁰Truly, truly, I say to you, you will weep and lament, but the world will rejoice. You will be sorrowful, but your sorrow will turn into joy. ²¹When a woman is giving birth, she has sorrow because her hour has come, but when she has delivered the baby, she no longer remembers the anguish, for joy that a human being has been born into the world. ²²So also you have sorrow now, but I will see you again and your

hearts will rejoice, and no one will take your joy from you. ²³In that day you will ask nothing of me. Truly, truly, I say to you, whatever you ask of the Father in my name, he will give it to you. ²⁴Until now you have asked nothing in my name. Ask, and you will receive, that your joy may be full.

I Have Overcome the World

²⁵"I have said these things to you in figures of speech. The hour is coming when I will no longer speak to you in figures of speech but will tell you plainly about the Father. ²⁶In that day you will ask in my name, and I do not say to you that I will ask the Father on your behalf; ²⁷for the Father himself loves you, because you have loved me and have believed that I came from God. ²⁸I came from the Father and have come into the world, and now I am leaving the world and going to the Father."

²⁹His disciples said, "Ah, now you are speaking plainly and not using figurative speech! ³⁰Now we know that you know all things and do not need anyone to question you; this is why we believe that you came from God." ³¹Jesus answered them, "Do you now believe? ³²Behold, the hour is coming, indeed it has come, when you will be scattered, each to his own home, and will leave me alone. Yet I am not alone, for the Father is with me. ³³I have said these things to you, that in me you may have peace. In the world you will have tribulation. But take heart; I have overcome the world."

Go Deeper

As He gave His final words of instruction at the Last Supper, Jesus focused on prayer and perseverance. He talked to them *about prayer* before He talked to His Father *in prayer* in chapter 17. But He made it clear that the ultimate purpose of prayer was not to give His followers the resources for a pain-free or problem-free life. Rather, the purpose of prayer is to maintain the peace that believers have in Christ.

Jesus' summary of His words during the supper was, "I have said these things to you, that in me you may have peace" (John 16:33). He had already promised the disciples peace as part of His gift to them. "Peace I leave with you; my peace I give to you. Not as the world gives do I give to you. Let not your hearts be troubled, neither let them be afraid" (14:27). But, as a powerful reminder of the kind of peace Jesus offers, He made the startling declaration, "In the world you will have tribulation. But take heart, I have overcome the world" (16:33).

The world can only guarantee trouble; Jesus promises peace. The world can promise peace it can't deliver. Only Jesus can deliver the peace to overcome the trouble we are sure to encounter in the world.

God's visit to earth changed time and eternity. Jesus is the center of history. His life fits like the final piece in the puzzle. Galatians 4:4–6 tells us Jesus came in "the fullness of time"—when time was ripe, at exactly the right moment. And He started a new way in which God relates with His creation. In John 16, Jesus continued to teach His disciples about the amazing personal resource that would soon be implanted in their lives.

Jesus' profile of the Holy Spirit is expanded in this chapter to add the role of "Convicter" to the role of Counselor. The Holy Spirit is God's convicting presence in the world. His arrival would signal two stepped-up functions: one for the world at large and one for believers. Jesus promised that when the Holy Spirit comes, "He will convict the world concerning sin and righteousness and judgment: concerning sin, because they do not believe in me; concerning righteousness, because I go to the Father, and you will see me no longer; concerning judgment, because the ruler of this world is judged" (John 16:8–11).

We often use the term "conviction" to describe those inward struggles that lead people to recognize the error of their ways. Conviction in this sense often leads to repentance (turning away from sin) and regeneration (turning toward God). Most of us know from experience, however, that conviction is not irresistible. We can clearly understand that we're about to do something wrong or have just done something wrong and yet refuse to repent. Jesus had a broader use of conviction in mind here, spelling out the Spirit's role in troubling the world about God and preparing the case that will lead to judgment.

The Holy Spirit convicts the world in three areas: sin, righteousness and judgment. Jesus provided a specific example for each of these areas of conviction. First, the Spirit warns about the ultimate sin of not believing in Christ (16:9). Rejection of Jesus cuts people off from the way of forgiveness and spurs on more sin. Without the Spirit's help, people would never grasp the danger ahead for those who refuse to acknowledge their need for a Savior.

"The Holy Spirit brings about a hunger for righteousness that spurs people toward repentance from sin and keeps us on the way when we are seeking to live for Christ. Christ's physical presence has been temporarily withdrawn, but the Holy Spirit functions as the constant GPS (God's Present Spirit), making us aware of God's character and desires."

Second, God's Spirit convicts the world about righteousness "because I go to the Father, and you will see me no longer" (v. 10). History demonstrates that our consciences fail in keeping us from sin and directing us to Christ. The Holy Spirit brings about a hunger for righteousness that spurs people toward repentance from sin and keeps us on the way when we are seeking to live for Christ. Christ's physical presence has been temporarily withdrawn, but the Holy Spirit functions as the constant GPS (God's Present Spirit), making us aware of God's character and desires.

Third, the Helper has the tough job of keeping the reality of coming judgment before the minds and hearts of the world. Jesus pictured the "ruler of this world" (v. 11) as already "judged." Satan's fate is sealed. Those who reject even the Spirit's work of conviction will eventually discover to their shock that they have at the same time been accepting a place alongside Satan when the final judgment is revealed. It would be a huge mistake to downplay the intimate role of the Holy Spirit in the daily lives of every person.

Jesus also promised that, "When the Spirit of truth comes, he will guide you into all the truth, for he will not speak on his own authority, but whatever he hears he will speak, and he will declare to you the things that are to come" (v. 13). These words had their immediate fulfillment in the disciples' producing the New Testament writings. John must have felt the special impact of the words "the things that are to come" many years later when he recorded the vision we call the Revelation of Jesus Christ.

But Jesus' words also apply to our lives as a promise of God's guidance. The promise doesn't discount our ability to refuse to follow, but God assures us that His Spirit will guide us "into all the truth." We have the freedom to pray King David's ancient words and find them even truer today than he was able to experience: "Where shall I go from your Spirit? Or where shall I flee from your presence?" (Ps. 139:7). As believers, we have a divine GPS with us everywhere we go!

Express It

Part of Jesus' instruction on prayer had to do with asking "in my name" (John 16:26). Our prayers rise to God wrapped in Jesus' name, with His authority and permission. This is why we often end prayers with the phrase, "In Jesus' name." It reminds us that we're not speaking to God based on our worthiness or importance but based on Christ's supreme position. In prayer, we walk into the Father's throne room holding Jesus' hand. As you pray today, keep that picture in your mind.

Consider It

As you read John 16:1–33, consider these questions:

1) Why did Jesus call His departure a benefit for the disciples?

2) In what ways have you experienced the work of the Holy Spirit in your life?

3) What evidence do you see of the Holy Spirit's work in the world?

4) How does the world's treatment of Christians and Christ's Church give a clue that the Holy Spirit is at work?

5) How did Jesus in this chapter further prepare His disciples for their future experiences?

6) What indications about His Resurrection did Jesus give in this chapter?

7) What comfort do you take from verse 33 in this chapter?

Lesson 17

On Jesus' Prayer List

What goes through your heart and mind when someone prays for you by name, out loud? How would it affect you to know that Jesus prayed for you? You have been on His prayer list and on His lips for a long time!

John 17:1–26

The High Priestly Prayer

17 When Jesus had spoken these words, he lifted up his eyes to heaven, and said, "Father, the hour has come; glorify your Son that the Son may glorify you, [2]since you have given him authority over all flesh, to give eternal life to all whom you have given him. [3]And this is eternal life, that they know you the only true God, and Jesus Christ whom you have sent. [4]I glorified you on earth, having accomplished the work that you gave me to do. [5]And now, Father, glorify me in your own presence with the glory that I had with you before the world existed.

[6]"I have manifested your name to the people whom you gave me out of the world. Yours they were, and you gave them to me, and they have kept your word. [7]Now they know that everything that you have given me is from you. [8]For I have given them the words that you gave me, and they have received them and have come to know in truth that I came from you; and they have believed that you sent me. [9]I am praying for them. I am not praying for the world but for those whom you have given me, for they are yours. [10]All mine are yours, and yours are mine, and I am glorified in them. [11]And I am no longer in the world, but they are in the world, and I am coming to you. Holy Father, keep them in your name, which you have given me, that they may be one, even as we are one. [12]While I was with them, I kept them in your name, which you have given me. I have guarded them, and not one of them has been lost except the son of destruction, that the Scripture might be fulfilled. [13]But now I am coming to you, and these things I speak in the world, that they may have my joy fulfilled in themselves. [14]I have given them your word, and the world has hated them because they are not of the world, just as I am not of the world. [15]I do not ask that you take them out of the world, but that you keep them from the evil one.

[16]They are not of the world, just as I am not of the world. [17]Sanctify them in the truth; your word is truth. [18]As you sent me into the world, so I have sent them into the world. [19]And for their sake I consecrate myself, that they also may be sanctified in truth.

Key Verse

"I do not ask for these only, but also for those who will believe in me through their word" (John 17:20).

[20]"I do not ask for these only, but also for those who will believe in me through their word, [21]that they may all be one, just as you, Father, are in me, and I in you, that they also may be in us, so that the world may believe that you have sent me. [22]The glory that you have given me I have given to them, that they may be one even as we are one, [23]I in them and you in me, that they may become perfectly one, so that the world may know that you sent me and loved them even as you loved me. [24]Father, I desire that they also, whom you have given me, may be with me where I am, to see my glory that you have given me because you loved me before the foundation of the world. [25]O righteous Father, even though the world does not know you, I know you, and these know that you have sent me. [26]I made known to them your name, and I will continue to make it known, that the love with which you have loved me may be in them, and I in them."

Go Deeper

Jesus' bold prayer for unity sometimes sounds hopeless in today's world. Even if we restrict the issue of unity to those who claim to follow Jesus and hold His Word in high esteem, the Church seems to be characterized more by cracks, brokenness and hostility. Are we any closer to seeing Jesus' prayer answered?

When we become a Christian, our personalities, tastes and styles may still be very different. Jesus didn't pray for unity in that sense. John 17 tells us that the unity Christ wants us to exhibit as believers is exactly the kind of unity that the Son has with the Father. That's *essential* unity; the unity of what we are, not the unity of personality. Believers are all born again by the blood of Jesus Christ. We may operate in the Body in different roles, but in essence we are the same. It's a unity based on what's central, not what's secondary, that's important.

Jesus prayed continuously. He was in constant communion with His Father, but He set specific time aside to speak with God. We know about these times because the disciples noted that He regularly slipped away for time alone.

Mark 1:35 introduces us to Jesus' prayer habit: "And rising very early in the morning, while it was still dark, he departed and went out to a desolate place, and there he prayed." We also know about the content of those times because He allowed the disciples to hear Him.

Eventually, the disciples asked Jesus to teach them. "Now Jesus was praying in a certain place, and when he finished, one of his disciples said to him, 'Lord, teach us to pray, as John taught his disciples'" (Luke 11:1). Jesus took the occasion to give them what we now call the Lord's Prayer. Isn't it interesting that the disciples didn't ask, "Lord, will you teach us to pray like You do?" Perhaps they were simply stating their understanding that rabbis customarily taught their followers how to pray. Or maybe they were so intimidated by the power and intimacy of Jesus' prayer life that they couldn't imagine being able to pray like Him. So, they asked for some basic prayer instruction.

Jesus not only taught them to pray; He invited them into intimacy with His Father. Because the opening words of the Lord's Prayer are so familiar to us, we may miss the earthshaking significance of "Our Father." Jewish people never addressed God in such personal terms. They hesitated even to say His name out loud, lest they use it in vain. Speaking to God as a child speaks to a father was probably strange and wonderful for those disciples. They received plenty of encouragement and examples from Jesus.

At the end of the Last Supper, Jesus "lifted up his eyes" and talked to His Father (John 17:1). We who are used to bowing our heads might from time to time benefit from lifting our eyes. Jesus began His prayer by reviewing God's eternal plan for humanity—to give fallen creatures the opportunity to "know you the only true God, and Jesus Christ whom you have sent" (17:3). He declared His disciples had reached a point where they knew three crucial facts: 1) "everything that you have given me is from you" (v. 7); 2) "that I came from you" (v. 8); and 3) "that you sent me" (v. 8). Although they would soon desert Him under extreme pressure, Jesus was confident His disciples already possessed what they needed for long-term spiritual survival.

Having said that, Jesus made several requests of His Father for His followers: 1) "keep them in your name" (v. 11); 2) "keep them from the evil one" (v. 15); 3) "Sanctify them in the truth" (v. 17); 4) "that they may all be one" (v. 21); and 5) "that they also, whom you have given me, may be with me where I am" (v. 24). What a powerful sequence of desires from Jesus' heart for His disciples—including us! Between His third and fourth request, Jesus described those He had in mind as He prayed: His disciples as well as "those who will believe in me through their word" (v. 20). If you are a follower of Jesus, you can point to a specific place in Scripture where Jesus prayed for you.

The word "keep" that Jesus used in verses 11, 12 and 15 can also be translated "protect." Jesus was "handing off" all His followers into His Father's hands for safekeeping. Because Jesus was confident of His Father's will in this matter, His prayer had the primary purpose of informing those overhearing Him. As

> " *If you are a follower of Jesus, you can point to a specific place in Scripture where Jesus prayed for you.* "

readers of the report of those disciples, we're included. Jesus prayed for our "keeping." The term "sanctify" in Jesus' third request can be read in several ways, but the common thread that runs through them is the teaching that God sanctifies (makes us spiritually healthy), and He does it through His Word.

Jesus' final two requests have to do with our relationship with each other and our relationship with Him. Jesus began and ended the Last Supper with our unity on His mind. First, He opened the evening by washing the disciples' feet, giving them a common experience and then asking to commit to serving one another as a witness to the world. In His closing prayer, He again asked the Father to make us one. The purpose of our unity would result in the world believing "that you have sent me" (v. 21).

Jesus prayed "through" us just as He prayed "through" the disciples. His request for us was not intended merely for our benefit but to help the process through which other people will come to believe in Jesus because they see what happens between us. Jesus wants others to come to know Him through you. How interested are you in seeing that happen?

Express It

Turn today's chapter into prayer by echoing Jesus' prayer. Start with the word "Father" from verse 1 and read the passage out loud, as Jesus prayed it. Add your personal comments, questions and requests as you follow Jesus' words. Make a note of the discoveries and decisions you make as you pray.

Consider It

As you read John 17:1–26, consider these questions:

1) What did Jesus say in this chapter about His authority from the Father?

2) Explain how Jesus seems to be using the word "glorify" in these verses.

3) Why did Jesus pray for His disciples (and us)?

4) Who was the sad exception to Jesus' protection and why?

5) What did Jesus want the world to know, and how would they best find out?

6) Based on this chapter, how would you describe Jesus' relationship with His Father?

7) What are some of the things that keep believers divided today? Why?

8) In what ways do you pray and work for unity with other believers?

Failed Intentions

Denial comes easily for many of us. We have something to hide, something we'd rather ignore or get away with. But what about denying a friend or acting like you don't know a family member? As you go through this lesson, ask yourself: Could you, would you, ever deny your faith in Jesus?!

John 18:1–40

Betrayal and Arrest of Jesus

18 When Jesus had spoken these words, he went out with his disciples across the Kidron Valley, where there was a garden, which he and his disciples entered. ²Now Judas, who betrayed him, also knew the place, for Jesus often met there with his disciples. ³So Judas, having procured a band of soldiers and some officers from the chief priests and the Pharisees, went there with lanterns and torches and weapons. ⁴Then Jesus, knowing all that would happen to him, came forward and said to them, "Whom do you seek?" ⁵They answered him, "Jesus of Nazareth." Jesus said to them, "I am he." Judas, who betrayed him, was standing with them. ⁶When Jesus said to them, "I am he," they drew back and fell to the ground. ⁷So he asked them again, "Whom do you seek?" And they said, "Jesus of Nazareth." ⁸Jesus answered, "I told you that I am he. So, if you seek me, let these men go." ⁹This was to fulfill the word that he had spoken: "Of those whom you gave me I have lost not one." ¹⁰Then Simon Peter, having a sword, drew it and struck the high priest's servant and cut off his right ear. (The servant's name was Malchus.) ¹¹So Jesus said to Peter, "Put your sword into its sheath; shall I not drink the cup that the Father has given me?"

Jesus Before the High Priest

¹²So the band of soldiers and their captain and the officers of the Jews arrested Jesus and bound him. ¹³First they led him to Annas, for he was the father-in-law of Caiaphas, who was high priest that year. ¹⁴It was Caiaphas who had advised the Jews that it would be expedient that one man should die for the people.

Peter Denies Jesus

¹⁵Simon Peter followed Jesus, and so did another disciple. Since that disciple was known to the high priest, he entered with Jesus into the court of the high priest, ¹⁶but Peter stood outside at the door. So the other disciple, who was known to the high priest, went out and spoke to the servant girl who kept watch at the door, and brought Peter in. ¹⁷The servant girl at the door said to Peter, "You also are not one of this man's disciples, are you?" He said, "I am not." ¹⁸Now the servants and officers had made a charcoal fire, because it was cold, and they were standing and warming themselves. Peter also was with them, standing and warming himself.

> # Key Verse
>
> *Peter again denied it, and at once a rooster crowed* (John 18:27).

The High Priest Questions Jesus

¹⁹The high priest then questioned Jesus about his disciples and his teaching. ²⁰Jesus answered him, "I have spoken openly to the world. I have always taught in synagogues and in the temple, where all Jews come together. I have said nothing in secret. ²¹Why do you ask me? Ask those who have heard me what I said to them; they know what I said." ²²When he had said these things, one of the officers standing by struck Jesus with his hand, saying, "Is that how you answer the high priest?" ²³Jesus answered him, "If what I said is wrong, bear witness about the wrong; but if what I said is right, why do you strike me?" ²⁴Annas then sent him bound to Caiaphas the high priest.

Peter Denies Jesus Again

[25]Now Simon Peter was standing and warming himself. So they said to him, "You also are not one of his disciples, are you?" He denied it and said, "I am not." [26]One of the servants of the high priest, a relative of the man whose ear Peter had cut off, asked, "Did I not see you in the garden with him?" [27]Peter again denied it, and at once a rooster crowed.

Jesus Before Pilate

[28]Then they led Jesus from the house of Caiaphas to the governor's headquarters. It was early morning. They themselves did not enter the governor's headquarters, so that they would not be defiled, but could eat the Passover. [29]So Pilate went outside to them and said, "What accusation do you bring against this man?" [30]They answered him, "If this man were not doing evil, we would not have delivered him over to you." [31]Pilate said to them, "Take him yourselves and judge him by your own law." The Jews said to him, "It is not lawful for us to put anyone to death." [32]This was to fulfill the word that Jesus had spoken to show by what kind of death he was going to die.

My Kingdom Is Not of This World

[33]So Pilate entered his headquarters again and called Jesus and said to him, "Are you the King of the Jews?" [34]Jesus answered, "Do you say this of your own accord, or did others say it to you about me?" [35]Pilate answered, "Am I a Jew? Your own nation and the chief priests have delivered you over to me. What have you done?" [36]Jesus answered, "My kingdom is not of this world. If my kingdom were of this world, my servants would have been fighting, that I might not be delivered over to the Jews. But my kingdom is not from the world." [37]Then Pilate said to him, "So you are a king?" Jesus answered, "You say that I am a king. For this purpose I was born and for this purpose I have come into the world—to bear witness to the truth. Everyone who is of the truth listens to my voice." [38]Pilate said to him, "What is truth?"

After he had said this, he went back outside to the Jews and told them, "I find no guilt in him. [39]But you have a custom that I should release one man for you at the Passover. So do you want me to release to you the King of the Jews?" [40]They cried out again, "Not this man, but Barabbas!" Now Barabbas was a robber.

Go Deeper

Pilate met King Jesus and was impressed, but not changed. John 18:28–40 records the encounter between the two men. Pilate tried to have Jesus released because he knew Jesus wasn't guilty of the charges against Him. But he was also a politician anxious to keep the "peace." When he came face-to-face with the Prince of Peace, he missed an opportunity to know true peace.

Like Pilate, the world sees Jesus as a good man, a teacher and a promoter of love, good deeds and the golden rule. Some see Him as a religious leader, the founder of the Christian religion. Others see Him as a threat and see all who follow Him as the enemy. Writers of literature often see Him as a pathetic figure, someone who was deluded, pitiful and, sometimes, a fool. Artists often picture Him as a sad sufferer on the cross, hanging there in pain for no good reason. To the world Jesus wears many titles, but King isn't one of them.

But Jesus claimed He was born to be king. His Kingdom is not temporal or worldly. He is the eternal king, the King of kings. What does it mean to you today that Jesus is King?

P eter was flat-footed. That doesn't mean he had to wear arch supports in his sandals. It means he was almost always off balance. Even his best efforts came off ill-timed.

Back in John 13, Peter blurted out a confession of steadfastness when he said, "I will lay down my life for you" (John 13:37). Jesus' prediction of his denial may have steeled Peter's resolve to stand with Christ. After all, he did try to defend Jesus with a sword when Judas brought the mob to arrest the Lord. But he only managed to demonstrate that a fisherman has no business pretending to be a swordsman. He was probably aiming to cut off Malchus's head but fortunately only lopped off an ear (John 18:10; Luke 22:49–51).

Shortly after his bold swordplay, Peter shrank from a servant girl. He had Jesus' warning, but he walked headlong into disaster. A mixture of fear, anger and insecurity contributed to his failure to acknowledge he knew Jesus. There's no indication that the servant's questions were accusations. They sound like curiosity. But Peter must have heard them as threats and responded instinctively—until the moment he heard the rooster crow.

With Peter's obvious failure on our minds, we might as well face the question, "Is it possible? Could we deny Jesus?" There's not much point in being concerned about what Peter did. But there's good reason to be concerned about what we do. Is it possible that you and I could do what Peter did? Could we deny the Lord? We won't ever be in a scenario like Peter's, set in the courtyard of the high priest's house, warming ourselves by the fire, awaiting word of what's going to happen to our Savior and Lord.

But there are similar scenarios that present themselves to us every day. First, we deny our Savior when we are silent to others about Him. That's what Peter did at the trial of Jesus. He didn't say anything; he didn't volunteer to be a witness. We don't either. Failure to communicate the love of Christ to our family and friends—that's denying Jesus. Psalm 107:2 urges us, "Let the redeemed of the LORD say so." Jesus said, "In the same way, let your light shine before others, so that they may see your good works and give glory to your Father who is in heaven" (Matt. 5:16). Peter stood by the fire, but he didn't let his light shine.

Second, we deny our Savior when our lifestyles deny that we have received Christ and are set apart to Him. The quintessential passage in the Bible about the lifestyle of those who do not deny the Lord is Romans 12:1–2: "I appeal to you therefore, brothers, by the mercies of God, to present your bodies as a living sacrifice, holy and acceptable to God, which is your spiritual worship. Do not be conformed to this world, but be transformed by the renewal of your mind, that by testing you may discern what is the will of God, what is good and acceptable and perfect." We deny our Savior when our lifestyles in the 21st century deny that Christ has transformed our lives. The world, rather than Christ, conforms us.

Third, we deny the Savior when our attitudes don't make others curious about Christ, our director. Paul said it this way in Ephesians 4:30–32: "And do not grieve the Holy Spirit of God, by whom you were sealed for the day of redemption. Let all bitterness and wrath and anger and clamor and slander be put away from you, along with all malice. Be kind to one another, tenderhearted, forgiving one another, as God in Christ forgave you."

We can say Jesus is our Savior, but if we're filled with bitterness, that bitterness is denying Jesus to the world. We're denying who we are. If we are kind and forgiving of what people do to us, they will wonder what makes us tick, who keeps us on balance. But when the world sees ugly attitudes in us, we deny the Savior. We do exactly what Peter did. It's just as easy to deny the Lord in the 21st century as it was in the first century.

" We can say Jesus is our Savior, but if we're filled with bitterness, that bitterness is denying Jesus to the world. We're denying who we are. "

Don't be casual about facing denials. If the examples above described parts of your life, let conviction do its work. Determine if you're denying Him by the way you live or the way you talk. And if you are, do some business with Him. Peter had to go and weep bitterly. There's little joy in discovering that you have been denying the One you claim to follow. Confess your denial, and ask Him to give you a second chance. He gave it to Peter; He'll give it to you too.

Express It

In this chapter, neither friend nor foe treated Jesus as King. But a genuine attitude of prayer requires that we think about Jesus as our King. Let Hebrews 4:16 shape your attitude as you pray today: "Let us then with confidence draw near to the throne of grace, that we may receive mercy and find grace to help in time of need."

Consider It

As you read John 18:1–40, consider these questions:

1) How did Judas know where Jesus would be?

2) What was the mob's reaction when Jesus identified Himself? Why?

3) What were the low points and highlights of Jesus' trial?

4) How did Peter get in the high priest's courtyard?

5) What questions was Peter asked that led to his denials?

6) What similar questions have you been asked unexpectedly?

7) Under what circumstances have you found it easy or hard to acknowledge Christ in public? Why?

Seeing the Cross

Two men on their way to two very different destinies. They were separated by a third man, all three of them on crosses. Even though two millenniums have passed since that event, one thing remains the same. How we respond to the One on the center cross will determine our destiny ... forever.

John 19:1–42

Jesus Delivered to Be Crucified

19 Then Pilate took Jesus and flogged him. ²And the soldiers twisted together a crown of thorns and put it on his head and arrayed him in a purple robe. ³They came up to him, saying, "Hail, King of the Jews!" and struck him with their hands. ⁴Pilate went out again and said to them, "See, I am bringing him out to you that you may know that I find no guilt in him." ⁵So Jesus came out, wearing the crown of thorns and the purple robe. Pilate said to them, "Behold the man!" ⁶When the chief priests and the officers saw him, they cried out, "Crucify him, crucify him!" Pilate said to them, "Take him yourselves and crucify him, for I find no guilt in him." ⁷The Jews answered him, "We have a law, and according to that law he ought to die because he has made himself the Son of God." ⁸When Pilate heard this statement, he was even more afraid. ⁹He entered his headquarters again and said to Jesus, "Where are you from?" But Jesus gave him no answer. ¹⁰So Pilate said to him, "You will not speak to me? Do you not know that I have authority to release you and authority to crucify you?" ¹¹Jesus answered him, "You would have no authority over me at all unless it had been given you from above. Therefore he who delivered me over to you has the greater sin."

¹²From then on Pilate sought to release him, but the Jews cried out, "If you release this man, you are not Caesar's friend. Everyone who makes himself a king opposes Caesar." ¹³So when Pilate heard these words, he brought Jesus out and sat down on the judgment seat at a place called The Stone Pavement, and in Aramaic Gabbatha. ¹⁴Now it was the day of Preparation of the Passover. It was about the sixth hour. He said to the Jews, "Behold your King!" ¹⁵They cried out, "Away with him, away with him, crucify him!" Pilate said to them, "Shall I crucify your King?" The chief priests answered, "We have no king but Caesar." ¹⁶So he delivered him over to them to be crucified.

> ## Key Verse
>
> *There they crucified him, and with him two others, one on either side, and Jesus between them* (John 19:18).

The Crucifixion

So they took Jesus, ¹⁷and he went out, bearing his own cross, to the place called the place of a skull, which in Aramaic is called Golgotha. ¹⁸There they crucified him, and with him two others, one on either side, and Jesus between them. ¹⁹Pilate also wrote an inscription and put it on the cross. It read, "Jesus of Nazareth, the King of the Jews." ²⁰Many of the Jews read this inscription, for the place where Jesus was crucified was near the city, and it was written in Aramaic, in Latin, and in Greek. ²¹So the chief priests of the Jews said to Pilate, "Do not write, 'The King of the Jews,' but rather, 'This man said, I am King of the Jews.'" ²²Pilate answered, "What I have written I have written."

²³When the soldiers had crucified Jesus, they took his garments and divided them into four parts, one part for each soldier; also his tunic. But the tunic was seamless, woven in one piece from top to bottom, ²⁴so they said to one another, "Let us not tear it, but cast lots for it to see whose it shall be." This was to fulfill the Scripture which says,

"They divided my garments among them,
and for my clothing they cast lots."

So the soldiers did these things, [25]but standing by the cross of Jesus were his mother and his mother's sister, Mary the wife of Clopas, and Mary Magdalene. [26]When Jesus saw his mother and the disciple whom he loved standing nearby, he said to his mother, "Woman, behold, your son!" [27]Then he said to the disciple, "Behold, your mother!" And from that hour the disciple took her to his own home.

The Death of Jesus

[28]After this, Jesus, knowing that all was now finished, said (to fulfill the Scripture), "I thirst." [29]A jar full of sour wine stood there, so they put a sponge full of the sour wine on a hyssop branch and held it to his mouth. [30]When Jesus had received the sour wine, he said, "It is finished," and he bowed his head and gave up his spirit.

Jesus' Side Is Pierced

[31]Since it was the day of Preparation, and so that the bodies would not remain on the cross on the Sabbath (for that Sabbath was a high day), the Jews asked Pilate that their legs might be broken and that they might be taken away. [32]So the soldiers came and broke the legs of the first, and of the other who had been crucified with him. [33]But when they came to Jesus and saw that he was already dead, they did not break his legs. [34]But one of the soldiers pierced his side with a spear, and at once there came out blood and water. [35]He who saw it has borne witness—his testimony is true, and he knows that he is telling the truth—that you also may believe. [36]For these things took place that the Scripture might be fulfilled: "Not one of his bones will be broken." [37]And again another Scripture says, "They will look on him whom they have pierced."

Jesus Is Buried

[38]After these things Joseph of Arimathea, who was a disciple of Jesus, but secretly for fear of the Jews, asked Pilate that he might take away the body of Jesus, and Pilate gave him permission. So he came and took away his body. [39]Nicodemus also, who earlier had come to Jesus by night, came bringing a mixture of myrrh and aloes, about seventy-five pounds in weight. [40]So they took the body of Jesus and bound it in linen cloths with the spices, as is the burial custom of the Jews. [41]Now in the place where he was crucified there was a garden, and in the garden a new tomb in which no one had yet been laid. [42]So because of the Jewish day of Preparation, since the tomb was close at hand, they laid Jesus there.

Go Deeper

When Jesus instituted the Lord's Supper on the night before He died, He created a way for His followers to "see" His cross. Interestingly, there is frequently a slip of the tongue made during communion when the bread is broken. It's easy to quote Jesus as saying, "This is my body, broken for you," yet that is not what Jesus said. He said, "This is my body, which is given for you" (Luke 22:19), or "Take; this is my body" (Mark 14:22), or "Take, eat; this is my body" (Matt. 26:26). There are some ancient manuscripts of 1 Corinthians that read, "This is my body which is broken for you," but the

(continued)

Go Deeper Continued ...

majority of texts read, "This is my body which is for you" (1 Cor. 11:24).

Why is this significant? John makes an important point in this chapter, and he highlights it with an Old Testament quote. When the soldiers came to break the legs of the thieves, which would cause them to die more quickly, they discovered Jesus was already dead. They checked by spearing His side. John notes, "For these things took place that the Scripture might be fulfilled: 'Not one of his bones will be broken'" (John 19:36). The bread is broken that we might share in it, not to symbolize a broken body. We take a small piece of bread and, seeing the cross, we remember the whole Christ is our Savior!

Crosses come in every shape, size and substance. Some are plain; others ornate. Some hang on church walls or perch on the tips of steeples. Many dangle from people's necks, and some from rearview mirrors. We see them everywhere. But few crosses today look much like the one upon which Jesus died. They are not ugly or rough enough. Who would want something grotesque adorning a sanctuary wall?

Unfortunately, the popularity of the cross comes with a lot of ignorance. Many people know what a cross is but don't know what it stands for. To them it might signify an attractive decoration or something "religious" that they can display on their walls or as jewelry.

This casual unawareness is miles from the robust and humbling words penned by Isaac Watts: "When I survey the wondrous cross, on which the Prince of glory died...." We have little doubt that Mr. Watts could *see* the cross. And he expressed what the New Testament consistently tells us, that the cross was significant because of Who died on it, what happened because of that death and what happened after that death.

Seeing the cross means meeting Jesus. Surveying the cross means not turning our eyes away from the love of the suffering Savior. Surveying the cross means listening for the brief statements Jesus made during His agony. John highlighted three of Jesus' seven "words" from the cross: "Woman, behold, your son!" … "Behold, your mother!" (John 19:26–27), "I thirst" (19:28) and "It is finished" (19:30). These statements capture both Jesus' humanity and His divinity. He took care of His mother, He felt deep needs and He finished His ordained task. And surveying the cross means remembering the stark difference between the two men who died alongside Jesus.

Was it just an accident that Jesus hung on the center cross? Was it coincidence that thieves were crucified on both sides? No; this makes much more sense as a God-incidence than a coincidence. It's part of the divine symbolism of the Bible. Every other human being is represented by one of those two men. One *trusted* in Jesus and received life. The other *mocked* Jesus and faced God's wrath.

Luke described the three-way discussion among the crucified men: "One of the criminals who were hanged railed at him, saying, 'Are you not the Christ? Save yourself and us!' But the other rebuked him, saying, 'Do you not fear God, since you are under the same sentence of condemnation? And we indeed justly, for we are receiving the due reward of our deeds; but this man has done nothing wrong.' And he said, 'Jesus, remember me when you come into your kingdom.' And he said to him, 'Truly, I say to you, today you will be with me in Paradise'" (Luke 23:39–43).

It was one of the fastest conversions in history. And the sinners did most of the talking!

Jesus was nailed to the cross between two thieves. He was on the center cross so He could reach both directions—reach to one thief and reach to the other. Jesus had already said, "And as Moses lifted up the serpent in the wilderness, so must the Son of Man be lifted up, that whoever believes in him may have eternal life" (John 3:14–15). He also said, "And I, when I am lifted up from the earth, will draw all people to myself" (12:32). Why was Jesus on the middle cross? He was there so He could reach out to *both* these sinners. He was there so He could reach out to you and to me.

"Seeing the cross means meeting Jesus. Surveying the cross means not turning our eyes away from the love of the suffering Savior."

But Jesus was also on the center cross because He separated the destinies of the two men on either side of Him. When you come to Jesus in the center, you leave Jesus one way or the other. One of the thieves left the cross to paradise, the other left his cross to hell. How each person responds to the invitation of the One on the center cross makes all the difference in the world. One cross portrays a thief dying *in* his sin. The other shows a thief dying *to* sin. But the one on the center cross shows a Redeemer dying *for* sin.

All of us need to come to the center cross to find the One who has been lifted up and is reaching out to us. And when we come to faith in Him, our destiny changes forever. If we go away from the cross like the thief who mocked Him, we go away *in* our sin. But if we go away from the cross today having trusted Jesus as the other thief did, we have the promise that we will be with Jesus in heaven. It's just that simple.

Express It

As you pray, take some time to gratefully describe what you notice when you see the cross. Tell Jesus what you appreciate about His sacrifice. Let the scene fill your mind, not in a morbid and gross way, but in a humbling realization of what it took to provide your freedom and open the way to paradise.

Consider It

As you read John 19:1–42, consider these questions:

1) Why did the Jewish leaders and the mob want Jesus to die?

2) How did the Roman soldiers treat Jesus?

3) What was the debate about the sign nailed over Jesus' head on the cross?

4) What do you "see" when you survey the cross?

5) How do Jesus' statements from the cross in this chapter strike you?

6) What did Jesus mean when He said, "It is finished!" (v. 30)?

The Empty Tomb

George Carey, a former archbishop of Canterbury, once said, "The Resurrection isn't central to Christianity. It is Christianity." Without the Resurrection, Christianity falls apart. It becomes at best another religion among many. As you go through this lesson, consider if you've settled this cornerstone issue in your life.

John 20:1–31

The Resurrection

20 Now on the first day of the week Mary Magdalene came to the tomb early, while it was still dark, and saw that the stone had been taken away from the tomb. ²So she ran and went to Simon Peter and the other disciple, the one whom Jesus loved, and said to them, "They have taken the Lord out of the tomb, and we do not know where they have laid him." ³So Peter went out with the other disciple, and they were going toward the tomb. ⁴Both of them were running together, but the other disciple outran Peter and reached the tomb first. ⁵And stooping to look in, he saw the linen cloths lying there, but he did not go in. ⁶Then Simon Peter came, following him, and went into the tomb. He saw the linen cloths lying there, ⁷and the face cloth, which had been on Jesus' head, not lying with the linen cloths but folded up in a place by itself. ⁸Then the other disciple, who had reached the tomb first, also went in, and he saw and believed; ⁹for as yet they did not understand the Scripture, that he must rise from the dead. ¹⁰Then the disciples went back to their homes.

Jesus Appears to Mary Magdalene

¹¹But Mary stood weeping outside the tomb, and as she wept she stooped to look into the tomb. ¹²And she saw two angels in white, sitting where the body of Jesus had lain, one at the head and one at the feet. ¹³They said to her, "Woman, why are you weeping?" She said to them, "They have taken away my Lord, and I do not know where they have laid him." ¹⁴Having said this, she turned around and saw Jesus standing, but she did not know that it was Jesus. ¹⁵Jesus said to her, "Woman, why are you weeping? Whom are you seeking?" Supposing him to be the gardener, she said to him, "Sir, if you have carried him away, tell me where you have laid him, and I will take him away." ¹⁶Jesus said to her, "Mary." She turned and said to him in Aramaic, "Rabboni!" (which means Teacher). ¹⁷Jesus said to her, "Do not cling to me, for I have not yet ascended to the Father; but go to my brothers and say to them, 'I am ascending to my Father and your Father, to my God and your God.'" ¹⁸Mary Magdalene went and announced to the disciples, "I have seen the Lord"—and that he had said these things to her.

> # Key Verse
> *Then Simon Peter came, following him, and went into the tomb. He saw the linen cloths lying there, and the face cloth, which had been on Jesus' head, not lying with the linen cloths but folded up in a place by itself* (John 20:6–7).

Jesus Appears to the Disciples

¹⁹On the evening of that day, the first day of the week, the doors being locked where the disciples were for fear of the Jews, Jesus came and stood among them and said to them, "Peace be with you." ²⁰When he had said this, he showed them his hands and his side. Then the disciples were glad when they saw the Lord. ²¹Jesus said to them again, "Peace be with you. As the Father has sent me, even so I am sending you." ²²And when he had said this, he breathed on them and said to them, "Receive the Holy Spirit. ²³If you forgive the sins of anyone, they are forgiven; if you withhold forgiveness from anyone, it is withheld."

Jesus and Thomas

24Now Thomas, one of the Twelve, called the Twin, was not with them when Jesus came. 25So the other disciples told him, "We have seen the Lord." But he said to them, "Unless I see in his hands the mark of the nails, and place my finger into the mark of the nails, and place my hand into his side, I will never believe."

26Eight days later, his disciples were inside again, and Thomas was with them. Although the doors were locked, Jesus came and stood among them and said, "Peace be with you." 27Then he said to Thomas, "Put your finger here, and see my hands; and put out your hand, and place it in my side. Do not disbelieve, but believe." 28Thomas answered him, "My Lord and my God!" 29Jesus said to him, "Have you believed because you have seen me? Blessed are those who have not seen and yet have believed."

The Purpose of This Book

30Now Jesus did many other signs in the presence of the disciples, which are not written in this book; 31but these are written so that you may believe that Jesus is the Christ, the Son of God, and that by believing you may have life in his name.

Go Deeper

This chapter makes the challenging and comforting point that believing is better than seeing. Thomas may have been the obvious "doubter," but he certainly wasn't the only one. His "demand for proof" was an expressed opinion that was likely held by the other disciples as well. The only difference for them was that they were there when Jesus first appeared in the room. Remember, John saw, and then he believed (John 20:8). Mary Magdalene saw, and then she believed (20:11–18). Thomas was simply expressing what the others felt, that until he saw Jesus in person, he could not believe. Jesus told all of them that believing is better than seeing (v. 29).

Later, the apostle Peter wrote to believers, "Though you have not seen him, you love him. Though you do not now see him, you believe in him and rejoice with joy that is inexpressible and filled with glory, obtaining the outcome of your faith, the salvation of your souls" (1 Pet. 1:8–9). Seeing isn't believing; believing is seeing. When you believe, that's when you see.

While honestly asking God for proof isn't wrong, it's just not the best that God has for us. Facts prove that we trust our understanding of what is truth. Facts are good. Faith is better. Believing is better than seeing.

Early Friday evening, Joseph of Arimathea and Nicodemus hurried to the cross with Pilate's permission and tenderly removed Jesus' body (John 19:38–42). They had little time because the Sabbath was about to start, and both men were devout keepers of the Law. Luke tells us that several women observed this process, so they knew where Jesus' body had been laid to rest (Luke 23:55). Apparently they felt the men probably hadn't done a complete job wrapping the body, so they planned to return after the Sabbath and give Jesus a proper burial.

John's account of the Resurrection morning only mentions Mary Magdalene, probably because she was the one who hurried to tell him and Peter about the empty tomb. But Matthew 28, Mark 16 and Luke 24 add Mary, the mother of James, to Mary Magdalene. Mark also adds Salome, and Luke includes Joanna, which indicates there may have been others. At least four women came to the tomb as dawn was breaking on the day that would change all of time and eternity.

The fact that the original witnesses to the Resurrection were women, and reported so, says a lot for the veracity of the account. If the Resurrection had simply been a rumor that was planted, it would almost certainly have been attributed to men, since women in that culture were not considered reliable witnesses. Apparently, God cares little for cultural rules that devalue people. If women are fellow heirs of the Gospel, they were certainly worthy to be the original witnesses of the empty tomb. The other Gospels fill in some of the details of this early morning shock when angelic beings instructed the women to spread the word that Jesus was risen from the dead. That's what the women did.

Urged by Mary Magdalene, Peter and John hurried to the tomb, which they found empty as she had reported. They believed something had happened, though they weren't sure what. John admits that he "did not understand the Scripture, that he must rise from the dead" (John 20:9).

Even after all of Jesus' hints and outright predictions, the disciples had to be convinced of His Resurrection. They didn't jump to conclusions about the empty tomb, and they didn't leap to faith. Mary Magdalene had to meet Jesus in the garden before she believed. At first she mistook Him for a gardener. Later that day, Jesus took the long walk with the two disciples on the road to Emmaus (Luke 24:13–35). Then He appeared to all the disciples (except Thomas) that evening. The Great Commission would not be declared for several weeks, but among Jesus' first words to His disciples was the order to go to the world with the news (John 20:21). One by one, Jesus' followers became convinced of the Resurrection. The empty tomb wasn't hard to prove. The meaning behind the emptiness was much harder to explain and accept.

Much-maligned Thomas is the poster child for those who find it hard to believe. They become fierce believers when they do believe, but they struggle to get to that place. Confronted with the account of the empty tomb and Jesus' visit to the other disciples, Thomas shrugged his shoulders in typical fashion and announced he needed more proof. "So the other disciples told him, 'We have seen the Lord.' But he said to them, 'Unless I see in his hands the mark of the nails, and place my finger into the mark of the nails, and place my hand into his side, I will never believe'" (20:25). He didn't think he could take someone else's word for the Resurrection.

Imagine for a moment what that intervening week was like. Was Thomas stubborn? Did he dig in his heels more each day in the face of the excitement of the other disciples? Or did he good-naturedly waver in his unbelief as he listened to the others describe their encounters with Jesus? By the time the next Sunday came, Thomas was ready to be proven wrong. When Jesus appeared, Thomas didn't waste time following through on his "proof strategy." He immediately acknowledged Jesus' lordship (v. 28).

> *" The empty tomb wasn't hard to prove. The meaning behind the emptiness was much harder to explain and accept. "*

This is another place in which Jesus spoke about us. He promised a blessing to those who don't insist on personal proof but are willing to believe without seeing. Those unwilling to believe often get stuck in prideful doubts. Jesus has given and will give enough reason to trust Him. When He does, are we willing to unashamedly say, "My Lord and my God"?

Express It

How often do you say to Jesus, "My Lord and my God!" as Thomas did? That spontaneous admission was also a confession. He stepped away from doubt and into belief. Jesus accepted his belief even as He pointed out that seeing shouldn't have been required. Thomas' words were also a prayer of submission. He went from doubting to ready for duty. "My Lord and my God" declares our willingness to accept God's commands. Make that your attitude as you approach God in prayer today.

Consider It

As you read John 20:1–31, consider these questions:

1) What explanations have you heard besides the Resurrection as a cause for the empty tomb?

2) What was John's original reaction to the empty tomb?

3) In this chapter, how did Mary Magdalene and Thomas react the moment they realized they were with the risen Christ?

4) How would you explain the significance of Jesus' statements to the disciples on the evening of Resurrection Sunday?

5) What were Jesus' greetings during His two visits with the disciples in this chapter? Why did He say that?

6) What is the connection between seeing and believing? How do they influence faith?

7) What did John say was his purpose in writing this book?

Lesson 21

Follow Me!

Like the elephant in the living room, Peter's denial remained a cloud over the joyous events of the Resurrection and subsequent days. It was a huge loose end that Jesus graciously tied up. If you've ever longed for restoration with God, here's your answer.

John 21:1–25

Jesus Appears to Seven Disciples

21 After this Jesus revealed himself again to the disciples by the Sea of Tiberias, and he revealed himself in this way. ²Simon Peter, Thomas (called the Twin), Nathanael of Cana in Galilee, the sons of Zebedee, and two others of his disciples were together. ³Simon Peter said to them, "I am going fishing." They said to him, "We will go with you." They went out and got into the boat, but that night they caught nothing.

⁴Just as day was breaking, Jesus stood on the shore; yet the disciples did not know that it was Jesus. ⁵Jesus said to them, "Children, do you have any fish?" They answered him, "No." ⁶He said to them, "Cast the net on the right side of the boat, and you will find some." So they cast it, and now they were not able to haul it in, because of the quantity of fish. ⁷That disciple whom Jesus loved therefore said to Peter, "It is the Lord!" When Simon Peter heard that it was the Lord, he put on his outer garment, for he was stripped for work, and threw himself into the sea. ⁸The other disciples came in the boat, dragging the net full of fish, for they were not far from the land, but about a hundred yards off.

⁹When they got out on land, they saw a charcoal fire in place, with fish laid out on it, and bread. ¹⁰Jesus said to them, "Bring some of the fish that you have just caught." ¹¹So Simon Peter went aboard and hauled the net ashore, full of large fish, 153 of them. And although there were so many, the net was not torn. ¹²Jesus said to them, "Come and have breakfast." Now none of the disciples dared ask him, "Who are you?" They knew it was the Lord. ¹³Jesus came and took the bread and gave it to them, and so with the fish. ¹⁴This was now the third time that Jesus was revealed to the disciples after he was raised from the dead.

Key Verse

Jesus said to him, "If it is my will that he remain until I come, what is that to you? You follow me!" (John 21:22).

Jesus and Peter

¹⁵When they had finished breakfast, Jesus said to Simon Peter, "Simon, son of John, do you love me more than these?" He said to him, "Yes, Lord; you know that I love you." He said to him, "Feed my lambs." ¹⁶He said to him a second time, "Simon, son of John, do you love me?" He said to him, "Yes, Lord; you know that I love you." He said to him, "Tend my sheep." ¹⁷He said to him the third time, "Simon, son of John, do you love me?" Peter was grieved because he said to him the third time, "Do you love me?" and he said to him, "Lord, you know everything; you know that I love you." Jesus said to him, "Feed my sheep. ¹⁸Truly, truly, I say to you, when you were young, you used to dress yourself and walk wherever you wanted, but when you are old, you will stretch out your hands, and another will dress you and carry you where you do not want to go." ¹⁹(This he said to show by what kind of death he was to glorify God.) And after saying this he said to him, "Follow me."

Jesus and the Beloved Apostle

20Peter turned and saw the disciple whom Jesus loved following them, the one who had been reclining at table close to him and had said, "Lord, who is it that is going to betray you?" 21When Peter saw him, he said to Jesus, "Lord, what about this man?" 22Jesus said to him, "If it is my will that he remain until I come, what is that to you? You follow me!" 23So the saying spread abroad among the brothers that this disciple was not to die; yet Jesus did not say to him that he was not to die, but, "If it is my will that he remain until I come, what is that to you?"

24This is the disciple who is bearing witness about these things, and who has written these things, and we know that his testimony is true.

25Now there are also many other things that Jesus did. Were every one of them to be written, I suppose that the world itself could not contain the books that would be written.

Go Deeper

The conversation between Jesus and Peter on the shore is one of the most intimate conversations recorded in Scripture (John 21:15–23). Here we see and listen as the Good Shepherd restores a sheep whom He has charged with special responsibilities for the rest of the flock. This sheep will be an undershepherd. Years later, when Peter was passing responsibilities for leadership to other believers, he used this same picture. "Shepherd the flock of God that is among you … being examples to the flock. And when the chief Shepherd appears, you will receive the unfading crown of glory" (1 Pet. 5:2–4).

While our English Bibles usually have Jesus asking Peter three times about the disciple's "love," the original language uses two different words in these questions. The first two times (John 21:15–16), Jesus asks about Peter's love in the ultimate, God's-kind-of-love sense. Peter can't bring himself to describe his love that highly. He settles for love in the deep friendship sense. Jesus' third question uses the same word for love that Peter used. He affirmed Peter's friendship and humility.

This dialogue becomes a helpful spiritual discipline when we take time to fill Peter's sandals and respond to Jesus asking us the same questions. How would you describe your love for Jesus? Is it sacrificial love or just friendship love?

Several lessons back, we noted Peter was flat-footed. Now he was crushed. During the events following the Resurrection, Peter, ever the first to open his mouth, was silent. When Peter visited the tomb (John 20:6–10), he never said a thing. The rooster's crow had been a hard lesson (18:27). In his account of the moment when Peter realized he had just denied that he even knew Jesus, Luke, always sensitive to the matters of the soul, tells us, "And he went out and wept bitterly" (Luke 22:62).

Now Peter didn't know what to do, but he had to do something. The only thing left that gave him any hope of normalcy and confidence was his old profession. So, he told the others, "I am going fishing" (John 21:3). He didn't invite them; they volunteered to go with him. We can only imagine the overwhelming feeling of helplessness as the night dragged on, and the nets remained empty. Peter may have felt as worthless as he had ever felt. He had failed his Lord; now he was a failed fisherman. He was looking for a small comfort in something familiar, but the chill of the night left him comfortless.

Then, out of the thinning darkness of the early morning, a voice called over the water, "Children, do you have any fish?" (21:5). They looked and saw a dim figure on shore. On cue, they chorused, "No." A stranger might have concluded these were some half-hearted fishermen after a poor night. Jesus knew better. His suggestion carried over the water with compelling authority. "Cast the net on the right side of the boat, and you will find some" (v. 6). These experienced fishermen must have thought, *What difference would it make? Still, what could it hurt?* They heaved the net and were amazed at their sudden change in fortune. The boat immediately creaked and tilted as the combined energy in a full net stretched the cords to the breaking point. They couldn't even retrieve the net, it was so heavy!

Wouldn't it be great to have the sound effects for moments like these? The grunts of surprise and the whoops of glee echoed from the boat. Perhaps Peter only felt relief and a glimmer of hope as he strained at the lines. Did he hear John laughing next to him, poking him and saying, "It is the Lord!" (v. 7)? How did he know? Jesus had done this before. (See Luke 5:4–11.)

Fish and success forgotten, Peter leaped to his feet. He jumped overboard and struggled to shore. Between the effort to get the boat to shore and the hilarity of watching Peter almost drown, the day began with a lot of excitement. But, curiously, Peter didn't know what to do when he reached the shore. He was completely soaked and shivering as Jesus probably led him to the fire and the smell of fresh fish on the coals. The others soon arrived, leaving the bulging net still in the water at the back of the boat near the shore. Restless and ill at ease, Peter immediately jumped up and rushed back to the boat and the overflowing net when Jesus asked for more fish to cook. They ate in stunned silence. No one knew what to say. All of them felt the weight of their recent unfaithfulness. Then Jesus beckoned Peter to walk with Him. And John, the disciple Jesus loved, eavesdropped on one of the greatest conversations of restoration in history.

As if unraveling the tangle of Peter's denial, Jesus asked him three times about his love. After each of Peter's answers, Jesus reaffirmed his future ministry by saying, "Feed my sheep" (John 21:15–17). Jesus even gave Peter a glimpse of the long years ahead before giving Peter a final, persistent command, "Follow me" (21:19). We can almost see Peter returning to his old self as he observed John behind them and asked Jesus about his future. "Lord, what about this man?" (v. 21). Jesus told Peter that was none of his business. Peter needed only to be obedient to the task Jesus had given him: "Follow me" (v. 22).

In a sense, the repeated commands, "Follow me," were Jesus' first and last personal words to Peter. Mark 1:17 describes Peter's original call to discipleship when Jesus said, "Follow me, and I will make you become fishers of men." This phrase captures a consistent part of our relationship with Jesus Christ. After

> **❝** *Our business, now, each day and always can be summed up in obedience to Jesus' words, 'Follow me.'* **❞**

we meet Him, we are asked to follow Him. After we fail, He meets us, restores us and asks us to follow Him. When we want to compare our journey with the journey of other believers, Jesus gently reminds us that's His business, not ours. Our business, now, each day and always can be summed up in obedience to Jesus' words, "Follow me."

Express It

Before you pray, stop to consider places in your life and relationship with Jesus that may need restoration. Jesus repeatedly said, "If you love me, you will keep my commands." Even if matters are "up to date" between you and the Lord, let Him ask you three times, "Do you love me?" and give Him some thoughtful answers in prayer.

Consider It

As you read John 21:1–25, consider these questions:

1) How do the words "follow me" describe your relationship with Jesus?

_____

_____

_____

2) In what ways do you relate with the disciples' helplessness and confusion in the days following the Resurrection?

_____

_____

_____

3) How did Jesus know about the fish?

_____

_____

_____

4) Why did Peter react the way he did to the news Jesus was on shore?

_____

_____

_____

5) How did Jesus' conversation with Peter serve to restore him?

_____

_____

_____

6) In what ways has restoration been part of your relationship with Jesus?

_____

_____

_____

7) What do you know about Peter and John's subsequent service for Christ?

_____

_____

_____

Purpose-Driven Writing

People who read the Bible attentively usually can't escape the impression that the entire Book and every part of it is purposeful. It came through the pens of many writers but had only one Author. John gives us a sense of how that driving purpose felt.

John 20:30–31

The Purpose of This Book

[30]Now Jesus did many other signs in the presence of the disciples, which are not written in this book; [31]but these are written so that you may believe that Jesus is the Christ, the Son of God, and that by believing you may have life in his name.

John 21:25

[25]Now there are also many other things that Jesus did. Were every one of them to be written, I suppose that the world itself could not contain the books that would be written.

Key Verse

But these are written so that you may believe that Jesus is the Christ, the Son of God, and that by believing you may have life in his name (John 20:31).

Go Deeper

John provides us with a beautiful summary of his purpose in writing the Gospel at the end of the 20th chapter. He did the same thing in his first letter. "I write these things to you who believe in the name of the Son of God that you may know that you have eternal life" (1 John 5:13). John wanted believers to be confident in their relationship with Christ. That confidence never flows from the quality of our faithfulness but from the immeasurable qualities of the One in whom we trust. Our confidence rests in His grace, not our merits. Paul described this confidence memorably in Ephesians 2:8–10: "For by grace you have been saved through faith. And this is not your own doing; it is the gift of God, not a result of works, so that no one may boast. For we are his workmanship, created in Christ Jesus for good works, which God prepared beforehand, that we should walk in them."

The life of a believer has two major chapters: life to the point of meeting Jesus Christ, and life following Jesus. Until we've met Him, we can't follow Him. After we've met Him, we are called to do nothing but follow Him. What chapter is Jesus writing in your life right now?

J ohn clearly stated his purpose in writing his Gospel at the end of the 20th chapter (see this lesson's key verse). There's a direct connection between the events of John 20:24–29 and John 20:30–31. The apostle used Jesus' encounter with Thomas to summarize the purpose of his writing.

Before describing the moving incident that ends this book, John wanted to make his message difficult to miss. He reminded us that his subject was inexhaustible: "Now Jesus did many other signs in the presence of the disciples, which are not written in this book" (20:30). He returned to this theme in the final verse of his Gospel (21:25). He also told us why he chose the events he recorded: "But these are written so that you may believe that Jesus is the Christ, the Son of God, and that by believing you may have life in his name" (20:31).

Having a purpose provides a crucial guideline for any effort, including writing. But having a purpose doesn't mean the same as accomplishing that purpose. Did John accomplish his purpose? Do we find in his Gospel all the necessary information and encouragement to believe "that Jesus is the Christ, the Son of God" (v. 31)? Countless witnesses through history have answered, "Yes!" Are you one of them?

John's purpose can be described as two steps. The first step involves the content of belief; the second step involves the results of belief. Believing in Jesus is never a static decision. It is a choice with legs on it. Trusting Christ transforms both life and eternity. In his purpose statement, John reminds us that "believing *that*" is not quite the same as "believing *in*." We can intellectually acknowledge that Jesus is the Christ, the Son of God, yet still not place our trust in Him. Throughout the Gospel of John, we have read illustration after illustration of people who believed Jesus was special, could do miracles and might even be the Son of God, but they didn't believe *in* Him.

The believing that John wanted to inspire in his readers was that whole faith that involves every part of life. It goes far beyond intellectual assent to a place of life-trust. When people like Nicodemus and the woman at the well met Jesus, their immediate lives took on a new direction. Jesus gave them something else to live for—the only One worthy of making that kind of demand. They literally got life in His name. Suddenly, they had purpose in life. Their existence from then on became defined by who He is. This pattern was repeated in the lives of the disciples and others along the way.

Even the writer of this Gospel, unwilling to name himself on its pages, underwent that transformation from belief *that* to belief *in*. Jesus' brother James described in his own letter the difference between recognition and trust when he wrote, "You believe that God is one; you do well. Even the demons believe—and shudder!" (James 2:19). Recognition is not the same as submission. Has John given us enough for saving faith in Christ?

John recorded a lot about the Savior, but what more could be said? If there were infinite time, if there were infinite space, if he had infinite ability—what more could John have said about the Lord he loved and followed to his death? Well, that's the right question. What's the right answer? Obviously, there is more than he could have said. John admitted that in the last verse of his Gospel. Just imagine all the teaching, imagine all the conversation, all the miracles and all the ministry that we have never heard about.

How foolish it would be for us to ponder the things that John had to leave out of Jesus' life and teaching and fail to appreciate the things he included! What a tragedy it would be to go verse by verse through this Gospel and yet miss the whole point! What John wrote, he wrote so that you would believe that Jesus is the Messiah of the Jews—so that you would believe that Jesus is the Son of God, and that by believing in Him, you would have eternal life in His name.

> *" What John wrote, he wrote so that you would believe that Jesus is the Messiah of the Jews—so that you would believe that Jesus is the Son of God, and that by believing in Him, you would have eternal life in His name. "*

Have you missed what this Gospel is all about? Have you missed the point of Jesus' life? Have you read, even studied, but failed to reach a place of personal trust *in* Christ? If you have, what's keeping you from believing in Him right now? John is the story of God's love for you. He sent His Son, Jesus, to die for you. That's what John 3:16 says. Jesus died on the cross in your place, to pay the penalty for your sin. Just like the one thief on the cross who believed in Jesus, you cannot only believe *that* Jesus is God's Son but you can move beyond that and receive the free gift of eternal life *in* His name. Have you done that?

Express It

As you pray, consider the lessons of the Gospel of John. Think about the mental pictures you gained of certain encounters with Jesus. Take time to thank the Lord for the ways He has touched and guided your life through your study of this Gospel. And be deeply grateful for the privilege to believe in Jesus, the only One who can save you.

Consider It

As you reflect on the entire Gospel of John, consider these questions:

1) What was your most compelling encounter with Christ in this Gospel?

2) How can the difference between believing *that* and believing *in* be illustrated in your life?

3) What have been some of the personal faith dividends you've collected in this journey through the Gospel of John?

4) What approach would you use in encouraging someone else to read or study the Gospel of John?

5) How many specific verses from John have you committed to memory? Why are they significant?

6) What would you say is the purpose of your life?

Notes

Notes

Notes